ONLY SLIGHTLY ASKEW

By Byron B. Long

Library of Congress Control Number:		2010913444
ISBN:	Hardcover	978-1-4535-7437-9
	Softcover	978-1-4535-7436-2
	Ebook	978-1-4535-7438-6

To order additional copies of this book, contact:
Xlibris Corporation
1-888-795-4274
www.Xlibris.com
Orders@Xlibris.com
84090

DEDICATION

I want to dedicate this book to my wife Angela for her love, support, suggestions and encouragement throughout the writing of these stories.

Also to my lifelong friend, Roger Kennedy, who provided the beautiful cover design for Only Slightly Askew, and who gave me inestimable help in guiding me through the steps of preparing the book for publication.

I don't want to achieve immortality through my work; I want to achieve immortality through not dying. I don't want to live in the hearts of my countrymen; I want to live in my apartment.

Woody Allen

Contents

ONLY SLIGHTLY ASKEW

Placebos

placebo *n.* a substance having no pharmacological effect but given to placate a patient who supposes it to be a medicine

I say phooey. I take placebos all the time, and I'm not fooled by them one bit, and I can assure you of this—they keep me fine-tuned and healthy. Anytime my stomach gets a little upset, or my nerves get frayed around the corners, I go to the medicine cabinet and take out a couple of placebos. They work like magic, and they're quicker than aspirin. Within twenty minutes, I'm like a new man.

Placebos have no side effects, and that's the unique beauty of them. It is axiomatic that if you take pharmaceutical pills for your heart, this will cause adverse side effects to your pancreas, kidneys, and liver. And if you have a problem with your hip, the pills you take will have a contrary impact on your knees, collarbone, and cranium. Every pill you take will affect you negatively in three areas of your body for every one that it helps. You can't avoid it. This was first discovered by the Greek physician Hippocrates who persuaded all physicians from then on to take an oath that they would observe and uphold this phenomenon.

I learned, long ago, that you can't purchase placebos in the drugstore. I tried to buy them from my friend Manny Laredo who is a druggist at the corner pharmacy. He said, "Are you crazy? You have to have a prescription to buy placebos." I told him I might go to Tijuana because I heard you could get them there—*no problema*—and for a song. Manny confirmed this. "That's true," he said, "and if you do go to Tijuana let me suggest that you locate the Mercado Primero and ask for Pepe. He carries them in thirteen flavors. If you see him, be sure to say hello for me because that will be worth a discount for you and a little something for me later on." Manny was quick to add, "Don't get me wrong, Pepe doesn't send me money, nothing like that, but at Christmastime, he does remember me with a pair of hand-painted maracas along with a pint of guacamole dip."

Before Manny went back to work, he told me he had nineteen pairs of maracas stored in his closet and that he hoped to unload them at a flea market during the next *Cinco de Mayo* celebration.

With Manny's advice in mind, I turned onto the Santa Ana freeway and headed for Tijuana. When I found the Mercado Primero, I went in and asked for Pepe. He emerged almost immediately from behind a phalanx of guitars that were hanging from the ceiling, and he banged into a few of them while walking toward me. I thought for a moment I heard a mariachi group warming up.

Right off I asked Pepe if he carried placebos, and he said, "Shhh," but then looked around and nodded affirmatively. I then asked him, sotto voce, in how many flavors, and he said thirteen. That's when I knew I had found my man. I placed a six months' order with him, and this almost caused him to smile, but he caught himself in time and instead scowled enigmatically. Then, while glancing furtively to his right and left, he sidled up to me and whispered, "Tell Manny he'll hear from me next Christmas."

Once again, I can safely recommend placebos to everyone. My favorite flavors (found through trial and error) are coconut sprinkles and olive mash, but all I suggest is that you try those two flavors first. And remember, there are absolutely no side effects, that is, unless you happen to be allergic to coconut.

Or, of course, to olives.

How High the Moon

The year 2009 marked the fortieth anniversary of the first human moon landing, and those of us who were alive then will always remember it. So much has been written about this great event, but as it turns out, there were many occurrences that were left unexplained by our government. I happen to have an uncle, Uncle Bibby, who still lives in Houston. He is a retired engineer from NASA headquarters, and he knows everything about the events leading up to the landing and its aftermath. He has generously offered to reveal the entire story, unauthorized but true, in this column.

First of all (Uncle Bibby said), there were four astronauts making the trip, not three as most commonly believed. There was the commander (pilot), and sitting next to him was the copilot who was in charge of maps and directions. Next came Neil Armstrong who huddled in the rear area where he spent the entire journey writing and rewriting the statement that became so memorable when he took his first steps on the moon. There was one more astronaut, and he appeared to be somewhat of a mystery. He had no accountable duties, and he kept whistling "Up, Up and Away" despite repeated threats to his body if he didn't stop.

So far so good. But there were little glitches, a few peccadilloes, and other assorted curiosities that plagued NASA during the early part of the mission. Here are a few examples: The commander worried incessantly that the moon, in a crescent phase at this time, would seriously reduce the lighted area for the spacecraft to land. NASA assured him that his concern was groundless, but that didn't seem to placate him. He also petulantly complained that his coffeemaker had shorted out during blastoff, and NASA engineers made many attempts to correct the problem through their computers—but failed.

Then when the craft approached the moon, Neil Armstrong came forward in order to practice reading what he had written—"One teensy step for man, one humongous leap for mankind." Upon hearing that, the commander immediately went into a holding pattern and told Neil that what he had written was great but to go back and give it one more rewrite. This took a while, so instead of the craft landing at 7:15 a.m. (moon time) as intended, it landed at 8:30, and the astronauts were grumpy because they had been in a "be ready mode" for hours, and now it was too late for them to enjoy their Weetabix and croissants.

Americans, and people around the world, were glued to their TV sets during this time, nervously awaiting the moon landing, knowing nothing about the above problems, and when the bumpy set-down finally took place, the Earth-bounders joyously cheered. That's when the revived astronauts emerged, golf clubs in hand, and Neil flawlessly gave his revised speech. Afterward, the men began bouncing up and down on the moon's surface, demonstrating the lack of gravity. They were a little worried that they might bounce up and not come down, but that didn't happen, as we all know. (Neil had wanted to be tethered to the spacecraft, but NASA convinced him it would make him look like a sissy, so he gave up the idea.) They continued bouncing until they developed a condition, fortunately temporary, known as vertical vertigo.

After a short rest and a return to normalcy, the astronauts proceeded with the scientific portion of their mission—collecting rocks. NASA, on top of things, had provided some egg baskets left over from the previous Easter. This seemed like great fun at first. But all they found were some granite shards and a few cloudy opals, too poor in quality to interest anybody at the jewelry mart. It was not long before they became bored with this endeavor, so after a short round of golf they shook the sand out of their socks, reentered the capsule, and were ready and eager to head back to Earth. The commander decided to follow the same route returning as coming, so the journey was rather humdrum, with nothing newsworthy to report.

Never explained, even to Uncle Bibby, was why the astronaut who had been whistling "Up, Up and Away" was missing when the craft reached the moon. Mysterious.

NASA's directors soon realized this man had never been listed on the flight roster, so they simply decided not to mention him. Problem solved.

The spacecraft had been scheduled to land at Cape Canaveral, but NASA (another glitch) didn't take into account that the flight was ending during spring break and that the tarmac would be crowded with happy, sober, fun-loving college kids. This forced the craft to reroute to Edwards Air Force Base in California, resulting in another jaunt around the Earth for the astronauts who were anxious to get home.

The craft finally touched down at Edwards in a blaze of glory, and the men waited, none too patiently, for the craft to come to a complete stop so they could unbuckle and alight. There to greet them were almost five hundred confetti and roach-tossing fans, the remnants of a rock concert that had been staged in nearby Palmdale the night before. The astronauts smiled at everyone—winked at the pretty girls—and bowed gratefully to those who threw their bras.

The men were then herded into a room where they were to be examined by a team of doctors who had had their medical training in Grenada. When told of the doctors' background, the astronauts managed to escape through a backdoor and go over to the Officers' Club where they began drinking beer, forgetting about getting home. Predictably, their levity crescendoed and then segued into barroom ditties with double entendres. They did this with gusto until the bartender, who was a born-again Christian (with perfect pitch), threw down his bottle cap opener, and stomped out.

Although stranded without further refills, the astronauts were undeterred and still euphoric because their mission had been such a huge success. They were also pleased because, according to their calendar, the following day was a free day, and this would enable them to participate in the Strawberry Pickers Protest March in downtown Oxnard, California.

They did so, and they would have been lost in the crowd of shouting, gesticulating protesters were it not for their chartreuse T-shirts which said on the back:

THE MOON IS GREAT—
IF YOU ARE A ROCK

At this point, Uncle Bibby became silent. After a while, he raised his eyes reverently and assumed a countenance of someone seemingly lost in the celestial. That's when I knew that his revealing and edifying story was concluded.

The Perils of Owning
a Restaurant

My name is Lindsay Abelard, and I am the "Dine Out" columnist for a California newspaper called *The Needles Desert Tortoise*. My column appears regularly, once a month in this paper and that is often enough, because Needles has just two small cafes and a Denny's to report on, each vying for distinction. However, because of my expertise, along with time to spare, I am frequently asked to go to Los Angeles in order to review the restaurant scene there. I would like to mention that I have my own way of rating restaurants—rating them by "spoons." Restaurants get from one to five spoons, with five being best.

One thing I observed while in Southern California this year was the large number of new restaurants that had closed for the age-old reason: lack of business. (I commemorated these now-defunct restaurants with a space in my *Desert Tortoise* column under the heading of "Frying Pan Heaven.")

The ones I wish to report on at this time were fine restaurants (all of them three to five spoons). While some of my readers contend that the names of these restaurants had much to do with their demise, I believe that it makes no difference what a restaurant is called as long as the food is exemplary.

Here were my favorites:

First, a place I thoroughly enjoyed was a sparkling little Jewish restaurant on Fairfax Avenue called *The Peanut Butter and Jelly Deli*. I thought its peanut butter was superior, but alas, it was gone in four months.

I lauded the Caribbean dishes at *The Fruit Fly*, a downtown eatery with a Jamaican ambience. It even tried to enliven its atmosphere with little buzzing sounds over the loudspeakers, but that didn't save it. It's gone.

Located in Venice was a modest favorite of mine (three spoons) a vegan delight called *The Rutabaga Bar and Grille*. It's no more. The owner's specialty was the blue plate special, Rutabaga Ragout, and it was scrumptious, although I did report that it contained a tad too much clove.

An expensive but good Italian restaurant called *Corleone's Coroner* closed in just three months to the day, and the intimate French restaurant, *Le Hot Vichyssoise*, the same. A four spoons steakhouse in Encino called *Tough Enough* had, even I admit, too trendy of a name, but it was otherwise excellent. Also gone. Next I discovered a praiseworthy Chinese restaurant in Monterey Park called *Oodles of Noodles*. I thought for sure it would be successful, but not so. It soon went into the red and disappeared.

Then there was a bold little Mexican restaurant in West Hollywood called *The Gay Ranchero*. It had a devoted clientele but not large enough to sustain the establishment. The manager told me the place only generated ten to fifteen percent of the business he had hoped for.

Finally, I found an upscale (five spoons) Polish restaurant in Beverly Hills called *Wzcyviezazki*. It only accepted telephone reservations, and I'm sorry to say, it closed in thirty days because not one person ever phoned in.

So there you have it, nine deserving restaurants—all of them now defunct—leaving me clueless as to why they failed to make the grade.

Noah's Ark, Early On

Rumors abounded for centuries that a young reporter had at one time interviewed Noah, an interview that reputedly took place just days before he began his Bible-detailed odyssey. In 1988, the story surprisingly turned out to be authenticated when the original account was discovered at about the 3000 feet level of Mt. Ararat, located on the border of Iran and Russia. It was in excellent condition because it had been sealed carefully in a bottle that appeared to be in blown glass, similar to carnival glass. In 1991, the contents were made available to scientists for scrutiny, and here for the first time is the actual account, revealed in its entirety.

"Good morning, Mr. Noah, my name is Jebbeth, and I'm a reporter for the *Jordan Times*. I've been hearing about the ark you've been building for the upcoming flood, and I wonder if I might ask you a few questions about your voyage plans."

"Voyage plans? Ha! Look, mister, I'm busy. This ain't no picnic, ya know, and I don't have no time for the likes of reporters. But what's your name again?"

"My name is Jebbeth, but please call me Jeb, and first of all, I want to compliment you on the completion of your exceptionally beautiful ark."

"Really? Ya think so? Well, I don't know, it ain't completed yet and it's getting jammed with more critters than you can shake a stick at, and all the while the Missus is after me because she's got no space for clothes. But I'm glad you like it okay, so I reckon I have a few minutes. Go ahead. Shoot."

"Thank you, sir. First of all, I understand you're taking a pair of every species of animal on Earth and putting them on your ark, the idea being to save them, while at the same time you intend to scuttle all the earthbound people in the process. Is that true?"

"Yer right on the mark about that, Jeb. As for the animals, hopefully, we'll get a male and female out of all the pairs, but I'm sure there'll be a screw up here and there, ya know how that is. But the people ya mention, well, they'll be goners. They're all bad news anyway, specially my neighbors. Trouble with them is, they party all hours of the night and they never turn out the lights or say hello. Yeah, they're gonna get deep-sixed okay and that's signed and sealed. But looka here, Jeb, I don't want you to think this whole thing is my idea. Just like you newspaper guys got bosses, well, I got a boss too and I do what I'm told. I'm a good soldier."

"I understand perfectly, Mr. Noah, so let's continue. I believe you have three sons. Is that correct, and if so what are their names?"

"Right again, Jeb, and their names are Shem, Ham, and Japheth. I named them myself, proud to say, and believe me, they're all great kids except they're worthless when it comes to shoveling out the ark. And of course, I have the Missus. Did I mention the Missus?"

"Yes you did. And how old are your sons?"

"Let's see, I'm 600 years old, won't be 601 till May, but I don't remember how old the boys are because their ages keep changin'."

"I would have the same problem, sir, but I'm sure you have a splendid family. By the way, are you managing to get the animals on board without too much difficulty?"

"No! In fact it's a royal mess. I never seen so durned many critters in my whole life. We started with the aardvarks six weeks ago, and this morning, we got the llamas on board, and it's my guess we're only about half way done. I ask you, Jeb, did you ever try to walk a pair of dinosaurs up the gang plank—especially when the two of them weren't getting along too good with each other in the first place?"

"I can sympathize, sir, but nevertheless you will still have the advantage over the rest of us because you'll be surviving and we'll be gone by the time you set sail."

"Aha! I got you there, Jeb, we don't have a sail—we'll just be bobbin' around. But I don't know, I reckon maybe yer the lucky one. I been told I can expect to live another 300 years, give or take a few, but my future ain't all that rosy 'cause my prostate is already startin' to act up."

"I'm very sorry to hear that, but tell me, how does the missus feel about the journey?"

"Terrible. She's already complainin' about the odors, and we ain't even left yet. Now she's after me to land in India when the waters go down so she can pick up some spices without it costing an arm and a leg."

"That sounds like good practical thinking on her part, Mr. Noah. Now I just have a couple more questions. Where will all the water that covers the Earth come from, and will it be fresh water or salt?"

"Hoo boy, now you got me, Jeb. Those are really stumpers, and I'm surprised at myself 'cause I ain't given it much thought to speak of. But I'll tell you what, I'll sure as shootin' look into it and get back to you if it's not too late. By the way, Jeb, I've been told we're only gonna be gone for forty days and nights, and you seem like a right nice young fella to me, so if yer of a notion maybe I could make an exception and get you stowed up somewhere on the boat. How 'bout it?"

"Thanks, Mr. Noah, but I must refuse your kind offer. I'm sure you realize that your mission is of biblical proportions and I wouldn't consider jeopardizing it for anything. But if you'll forgive me, I must hurry back to the *Times* and get my story in before the waters begin to rise."

"Okay, Jeb, I guess maybe yer right about not taggin' along, but now I've gotta scoot too. Got a couple of mammoths waitin' to board, and behind them are the mice, and after that come the monkeys. And I gotta feelin' them monkeys are gonna be a handful."

Molly

She was young and attractive, but she was not beautiful, at least not in the commonly considered sense of the word. Yet every man who knew her, and there were so many, would believe to the end of his days that she was the most beautiful girl they had ever known.

Molly, and that was the only name anyone ever knew her by, possessed an aura of innocent charm that was unusual for someone in her chosen line of work. No man was able to fully define the appeal of Molly, but undeniably, men were drawn as close to her as the wind to the sea. Her skin was light and almost translucent, the whiteness heightened by the lack of sunlight that was her lot for working through the night and sleeping by day.

Men would oftentimes come to her before their allotted time, knocking on the door of her room, and when they did, she would call out, "Please wait quietly by the door." She would then repeat the words with the same lyrical cadence in her voice, "Please wait quietly by the door." Men interpreted her words not as an admonition, but by the way she said it, as a soothing call to them. She somehow managed to convey to each man that she preferred him to the man who was now inside her room, and he would then await his time.

This was Saint Louis, Missouri, and it was during the waning years of the nineteenth century. Molly worked in an establishment that was typical of so many other places throughout the country. It was a business run by a strong lady who knew how to satisfy her patrons, and who, by unsubtle machinations, managed to make deals with the law that would allow her to keep her business operational. It was a time-honored, if not honorable, system.

As was common in those days, the lady had a piano player who played downstairs in the gathering area, the living room of a converted residence. He was a man of color and he played so very well, playing a music that was new, with a pulsating left hand, playing in stride style while his right hand veered off, seemingly independent, inserting darting syncopations that had never been heard before. The music was ragtime, although it would be a while before it would be known by that name. He played for long hours into the night, but even when his hands ached, the beat never flagged. His music, however, was forbidden elsewhere. It was the music of the "devil," banned in "proper places" because of where it was born and cultivated. It was castigated through the week in the newspapers and again on Sundays from the pulpits, and thus, many years were to pass before it would be considered an acceptable form of American music. By that time, the newness and the ardor for it had long been quelled. But not the appreciation of it.

Molly loved the music. It was, in fact, the only pure enjoyment that she had in her highly structured, constricted life. She liked most of all to be downstairs, to be able to socialize with the patrons and the other ladies, but all the while her inner self was absorbing the music. Even when she was upstairs, the music was palpable, though muted, and she could still sense its intensity, and it gave her life a meaning. Its only meaning.

Molly lived her short life unmarked by major events. For some time, she was the most requested lady of the house, and while the other ladies were jealous of her popularity, she still had that rare quality to be accepted and liked by both men and women.

Six years elapsed and around that time, Molly's looks began to fade, prematurely but perceptibly, and her seductive call, "Please wait quietly by the door," was heard less and less.

When she had only one more year to live, she became ill and was forced to leave the only home she had ever known.

Molly died at age twenty-seven, and when she died, she was alone and openly mourned by no one. But silently, individually, she was mourned by all who had known her. The Saint Louis newspapers recorded no mention of her death, and even if they had, it would have been unthinkable for them to have revealed the cause of her demise.

That's What Friends Are For

My friend Bumpy called me the other day and said he was planning on becoming a bartender. He wanted to know if I could give him some advice. I told him that I have been in lots of bars but I didn't know anything about tending bar. I tried to explain that I didn't know the difference between a cocktail umbrella and a swizzle stick—so how could I possibly help him?

"You know lots of different things, Eddie," he said, "so just let me ask you a few questions. For example, if you're a bartender and you're busy, what do you do if a customer starts talking to you?"

"Well, I can tell you what happened to me," I replied. "One time, I started talking to a bartender who was, like you say, busy, and he stopped me in mid-sentence and then told me a long shaggy dog story. At the end, I resumed talking. He just held his hand up and began the story again from the beginning. I got the message and clammed up. That freed him to take care of his other customers, and he came back later, shook my hand, and thanked me for being so considerate."

"You see, I'm learning already," Bumpy said. "By the way, do you know how to make a Gibson?"

"No, I don't, but I think they put an onion in it."

"I heard they put a twist of ginger in it too," Bumpy said. "Is that true?"

"Absolutely not, Bumpy, someone's pulling your leg, and I don't mean right or left. But I've heard that at the Hotel Persiflage in Beverly Hills they use an atomizer and spray a hint of *eau de vanilla* onto every *creme de menthe*."

"I'll write that down so I don't forget it. And now I have just one last question. Do you know what kind of wine people serve after having martinis, red or white?"

"That's easy," I said. "It's white. Martinis are white and so, of course, is white wine. Remember this rule! You don't ever mix colors with your drinks."

"You're a prince, Eddie, you've helped me a lot."

"Anytime, Bumpy, anytime. That's what friends are for."

A Love Letter

A letter was recently discovered that was written on July 16, 1580, by William Shakespeare and addressed to a lady acquaintance of his in London. Unfortunately, her name was smudged out, almost certainly by an irate Anne Hathaway whose fingerprints were to be found throughout. Regardless, the epistle has now been authenticated by the style of writing and turns of phrases that are recognized worldwide as pure Shakespeare.

To my Dearest (smudged),

Oh, my bloomin' little poppy petal, how I long, long, long to have thee share my pillow on this, the twelfth night of a lingering tempest. But thee is elsewhere, my sweet bon bon, so now while London sleeps I sit at my desk in my lonely loft, working on my latest play while my mind drifts, dwelling on thee, only thee. I am writing by candlelight—burning my candles at both ends—running out of candles—and all the while my rent is five, ten, maybe twenty fortnights in arrears.

I know nothing of fortnights, but I understand arrears, and in addition, my meandering lil' moonbeam, I tremble because

I fear that I am not worthy of thy favors. My all-consuming desire is to hear thee tapping delicately at my door with thine own sweet knuckles, imploring me to thrust it open and to sweep thee lustily into mine craving arms.

Oh, my pet potted petunia, I can never forget the night we swam the Thames, racing to get to Ye Olde Duck Pond Pub for an evening of unbridled merriment. I blush with vanity for saying I was far ahead of thee in our spirited endeavor, but, to my chagrin, that only lasted until my writer's cramp flared up, at which time I gradually slowed, only to lose by a trifle.

But our night at the pub was exhilarating. I was entranced and mesmerized by the candlelight shimmering on our foam-capped pitcher of ale. And thou wast dazzling, dressed in a crimson hopsack gown that revealed flashes of kneecaps when thouest danced on the tabletop—whirling dervishly to the sensuous rhythms of a hot gavotte.

Afterward, with unfettered anticipation, we glided lightheartedly o'er the cobblestone streets of our foggy London town, and arrived none too soon at the antiquated steps that led to my loft. We climbed and upon entering, I admit that I lost all gentlemanly control of myself. But because of the number of steps (seventy-nine), and my lack of adequate sustenance (due to the stacking up of my unsold plays), I weakened and can only remember fumbling clumsily with thine garments, unable to dislodge them because of their devilish catches—only to fall asleep with mine head upon thy ample bosom. At least, all was not lost.

Oh, my cheerful little earful, how I treasure another time when I kissed thy toes and thee wiggled them and squealed with innocent delight. Alas, that caused me to develop a foot fetish, and that kind of fetish is so difficult to rid one's self of. I was finally cured after five costly trips to mine foot doctor, Dr. Marlowe, who, after much haggling, agreed to accept a dusty old play of mine (Hamlet) as payment. But why did our lovemaking have to begin and end with thy toes? I realize that something is amiss, but I know not what, and I am so miserable I could die. Do only men get foot fetishes?

At this moment, dreaming of thee, I am besieged with images of flowers that churn like butter in mine fertile and feverish mind. They go like this: Thou art mine beaming sunflower, lighting the underworld beyond the tide pools of everlasting yearning. Thou art mine pale yellow jonquil, subtly climbing, climbing, to the rafters of an unknown golden shore.

Yes, these outpourings, a part of mine genius that is impossible to fathom or explain, are causing my brain to become a cauldron of feelings that can only be fully expressed by writing. And that I must do now—possibly in iambic pentameter—because, I am told, that is what sells better.

Yes, I feel a sonnet aborning, so please forgive me, my cute little cuckoo, while I suspend all thoughts of love and once again write with posterity in mind.

I remain thy devoted, but woefully unrequited,

Willy S.

Forty-eight Hours

It is well-documented that on September 2, 1945, General Douglas MacArthur, aboard the USS Missouri, represented the United States when the peace treaty marking the end of World War II was signed. MacArthur was scheduled to meet with Japan's ministers to conduct the ceremonies, but what is not well known is that Hideki Tojo unexpectedly presented himself forty-eight hours before the signing and declared that he, as prime minister, had the right to represent the Japanese. The ensuing drama became muddled at that time and has not been fully and accurately chronicled until now.

It was a historic event that should have proceeded smoothly according to the Geneva Convention's protocol, but problems surfaced immediately when MacArthur and Tojo were not able to agree on the shape of the table around which they would be sitting. After much haggling and wrangling, they finally decided an oval table would be satisfactory. But the *Missouri* did not have an oval table, so the carpenters on the mighty battleship solved the problem by cutting a round table in half and placing planks in the center to make it oval. Then some oilcloth from the mess hall was placed over it, and that gave the table a pleasing-enough appearance. All of this took six hours, but at least the talks were able to proceed.

Tojo immediately attempted to manipulate control of the proceedings by expressing his displeasure over the smoke emanating from MacArthur's corncob pipe. Pointing to his chest, he said he had asthma and began wheezing and coughing uncontrollably, and between coughs he recited the history of his problem. MacArthur stiffened and was clearly irked by this ploy, but he relented and handed the pipe to a staff colonel. He in turn handed it to a captain who handed it to an orderly, and he snuffed it out with his thumb.

During the ensuing talks, the pipe disappeared and when MacArthur asked to see it, it could not be found. He became morose, folded his arms and adamantly refused to continue until a replacement could be had.

Corncobs were rare in Japan at that time, and the embarrassing problem held up the talks for another eighteen hours while everyone waited for a plane that was immediately dispatched from Kansas bearing a corncob. A full day had now been lost.

Talks resumed when the corncob arrived, but this time MacArthur took command and made it clear that Emperor Hirohito could no longer be considered divine. Tojo strenuously resisted, calling this a sacrilege, arguing that divinity is divine by definition and therefore not negotiable according to the whims of mere mortals.

Regarding divinity, it might be noted that Hirohito had questioned his own divinity early on. As a boy he would say to his parents things like, "If I am a god why do I have to eat white rice

like everyone else when I would prefer to have pasta pomodoro?"
They would tell him to hush and, in effect, not to rock the boat.
And then they would box his ears hoping to knock some divinity
into his head

MacArthur was understandably upset by Tojo's position on divinity but he couldn't figure out how to handle it, so he decided to call President Truman for a solution to the problem. Truman told him the whole kit and caboodle was just a lot of B.S. and to get on with the proceedings and not to bother him anymore because he was busy helping his daughter plan her budding singing career.

MacArthur relayed Truman's answer to Tojo who indicated he understood the meaning of kit and caboodle but that he was still confused about B.S., so he waited while a subordinate looked it up in a Japanese dictionary. In the meantime, Tojo softened noticeably and with misting eyes said that his own daughter liked to sing and she hoped to go to Hollywood someday.

In this moment of sublimity, Tojo said he was willing to concede the issue of divinity, but how about the Spanish Inquisition, was that divine? MacArthur exploded and, while pounding the rickety table, emphatically stated that that was totally irrelevant. Tojo, who was now regaining steam, said okay, but how about the Vatican's claim that our Earth is the center of the universe?

That seemed to stop MacArthur. He called for a recess so that he could put in a call to the Vatican for clarification. Officials there told him how that church edict had been reevaluated at least a hundred years ago, and they archly suggested that Tojo should update himself on documented church history.

Another impasse in the negotiations was averted when the Vatican, at MacArthur's brilliant suggestion, offered a proposition that they hoped would facilitate the garnering of Tojo's signature. They dangled a carrot in front of him by saying that a revelation had just occurred to the effect that Catholics would no longer have to eat fish on Friday. This proclamation, the Vatican further stated, would only be issued if Tojo would sign the treaty. This seemed to mollify Tojo who, in his mind, thought that would mean more sushi would therefore be available to the Japanese on Fridays.

Nevertheless, Tojo in a delaying move asked if this was indeed a revelation or just a proclamation, and MacArthur, already in a dour mood because his Kansas corncob was smaller than his old one and not yet broken in, shouted, "It doesn't make any difference for Christ's sake, just sign it."

Tojo continued to waver and said he would not sign until he was guaranteed that the extra sushi available on Fridays for his countrymen would include shrimp and lobsters. When assured of this he smiled, borrowed a pen, and signed.

Everyone immediately rose from the oval table, shook hands, and hugged each other with great élan. A celebration was called for and before long a case of sake, labeled—For Medical Consumption Only (in Japanese)—manifested itself and was soon flowing like champagne. Even General MacArthur uncharacteristically mellowed. He climbed onto the tabletop and did a short Scottish jig and then generously granted a request by Tojo to have an extra bottle of sake to take home with him.

The war was now officially over and the peace treaty was hailed by everyone except for those in Japan. But it was dimmed somewhat for President Truman, because his daughter had just given her heralded concert and it was panned mercilessly by a Washington music critic. And Truman was busy penning a letter to the critic, giving him a colorful piece of his mind.

The Jewel

I had been divorced for nearly five months and was still in recovery, trying to find my compass while not succeeding very well. One day, I impulsively decided to get away for a week by traveling to Cairo, Egypt. Why I chose Egypt is beyond me—it was almost like closing my eyes and pointing to a place on a map—with my finger landing on Cairo. In retrospect, I believe there was a higher order making the decision for me—but I didn't know that at the time—and I will explain what I mean later.

I was a film editor by profession, having worked at Paramount Pictures for twenty-eight years before retiring. My work had always been relatively stable considering the seesaw nature of my profession, but my marriage, unfortunately, had been more buzz saw than seesaw. It progressed jaggedly and finally imploded, ending a relationship that had definitely not been, as my wife and I first vowed, made in heaven.

Cairo, when I arrived, was hot as expected. After I checked into the El Kahn Hotel, I spent the rest of the day trying to get my circadian rhythms in synch with the rest of me. I walked around the city, savoring the atmosphere which was totally different from anything I had ever experienced. I stood along the Nile which runs through the center of the city and enjoyed watching the variety of boats that plied that great river.

On the second day, I caught a city bus just for the experience of it, and yes, it was an experience. It seemed like five hundred people shared my idea, and the air was rife with the pungent aroma of sultry bodies. Sardines had it better than I, and I put my hand in my pocket, strangling my wallet just to make sure it didn't leave me.

On the third day, I decided to take a tour of the pyramids. I was Joe Tourist all the way and even mounted a camel and let a man walk the animal in a circle a few times while an aide took an obligatory picture of me. The man then issued his stock joke, "My camel, he is dizzy, and we must stop now." And of course, I was strongly encouraged to buy the picture.

The following day, I went to the National Antiquities Museum, a must for me even though I was not in any sense an archaeology buff. (My only expertise consists of an ongoing subscription to National Geographic.) Still, I wanted to see the relics, and they turned out to be more impressive than I had believed likely.

At one point, I stopped in front of a glass-covered tray of gemstones that had been recovered from an excavation. One stone in particular caught my eye. It was a sapphire of the deepest blue, and while it was not the largest jewel on the tray, the facets of the gem seemed to produce a light of their own, dominating the other stones around it. For some strange reason, I felt drawn to it magnetically, as if by an unyielding force.

That, to my normally logical style of mind was irrational, at least I felt that way at first, and I left the museum immediately—with an unsettled feeling. That night, I dreamed that the sapphire was telling me I had had a former life in ancient Egypt. This was not unusual for a dream, but when I awoke in the morning, I found myself half-believing it.

Let me say at this point that I had no history of unconventional thinking. I had always found feng shui and Shirley MacLaine to be quite humorous. Reincarnation to me was something that had no basis in fact and, of course, could not be scientifically proved, or so I thought. But here I was, phasing in and out of just such thinking; at times "remembering my past"—and starting to conjure details from a remote, ancient time.

I felt compelled to return to the museum hoping to dispel the demons that were beginning to pursue me, but upon approaching the jewel, its effect on me was just the opposite. It spoke to me, just as it did in my dream, and when I heard its voice, I became irrevocably convinced that I had been in truth reincarnated.

Today, a year later, I belong to a semi-religious group called "We're for You" that has some similarities to other self-help groups that I won't name. We have weekly meetings, but we get together more often than that. My new friends have been a big help in their ability to corroborate the findings of my previous existence through extensive religious tracings of my forebears. As a matter of fact, they call me daily to show and confirm their support. I have donated two thousand dollars to the organization so far, and I have come to understand its need for more so that it can continue its good work. I resisted their requests to turn my home over to them, but they were very persistent. I am now happy to be living elsewhere while they use my home as headquarters for recruiting adherents.

My former friends have urged me to be cautious and claim this group is nothing more than a questionable cult. However, I don't share their convictions. Unfortunately, our disagreements have escalated to the point where we seldom have contact anymore, mostly because of their inability to discuss anything rationally.

Finally, after all the changes that have taken place, I am at a time and place in my life where I feel peaceful, content, and better about myself than ever before. What is most gratifying is my newfound knowledge that I, without question, once lived in ancient Egypt. It doesn't matter to me (as it may to some) that in my previous life my lot was a modest one—beginning as a camel driver's helper while progressing to become a camel driver. It has been proven that the Egyptian sun god, Ra, is all-knowing, loves everyone, and considers everyone equal, regardless of his or her station in life.

When Astrology Meets Feng Shui

I'm always trying to do things to better myself. It's my nature, I suppose, but at the same time, I have a record of failures that appear to be disproportionate to my seemingly laudable aims.

For example, not too long ago I became interested in the occult, and I searched for and found a lady spiritualist who was quite accurate in her observations about my past. But when I asked her about my future, she hesitated and then said she could help me communicate with the dead. I accepted her offer and during her seances she did manage to connect me with some of my long deceased relatives. But I soon wearied of that because all they wanted to talk about was their health while they were on Earth and how they had nothing to do now and were bored silly. They wanted to see me, though, and said they couldn't wait for me to join them.

After a short hiatus from that frustrating experience, I turned to an Ouija board for guidance and it suggested that an astrologer might help me. Luckily I found a good one and he read my horoscope by calculating the conjunctions of the stars and the planets, then aligning them with the moons of Jupiter. That made me feel really good, so proud to be such an integral part in the scheme of the universe.

My astrologer explained that he always confirmed his findings by reading tea leaves (Oolong). He predicted, among other things, I would spend my summer vacation in Las Vegas. Unfortunately, financial problems forced me to settle for Sparks, Nevada, and that proved quite disappointing. My astrologer blamed his prediction on one of Jupiter's moons which, he said, was a tad out of alignment.

When I returned from my vacation, I was beginning to have some doubts about my quest for betterment, but that's when a good friend told me about feng shui. It's the ancient Chinese system of achieving harmony and well-being through the proper placement of your home and objects within. I was intrigued, and at first, I felt renewed.

That's when I decided to have a feng shui expert, a Chinese man, come to my home and assess it for harmony and balance. I thought he would like my home, but as it turned out, he was not at all pleased with what he saw. He told me my house had too much cha. (This is feng shui for negative force.) He said my back door should face north instead of west and that my flower pots were all placed wrong.

Rearranging the flower pots was easy but having the doorway moved and replastered cost me almost three thousand dollars. This resulted in my experiencing serious cha. When my feng shui expert reviewed what I had done to my house, he said it still wasn't right and that the whole foundation was out of kilter. It needed to be shifted toward the south in order to let more light in. Fortunately, he knew of a good contractor who was able to save me some money doing it.

I was quite confused by this time but that's when I had what I thought was a good idea. I asked my astrologer to meet with my feng shuiist and have the two of them straighten out some of the contradictions in their theories. They did meet, but when I went to my astrologer the following day, I noticed he was a bit hunched over and walked with an observable limp. I asked him what happened at their meeting and all he said was that my feng shuiist had to be the only Chinese sumo wrestler in the entire world.

At this point in my life, I have become very depressed, and I am totally lacking in harmony and balance. I have lots and lots of cha, and I don't know who to turn to or what to do.

Come to think of it, I have heard about a clairvoyant in Hollywood who is reputed to be quite good. Better yet, I think I'll just pick up a deck of tarot cards and figure all of this out for myself.

Zeus, Then and Now

There are not many followers today of the Greek god, Zeus, the icon who was once considered to be the supreme being of the universe. However, at the risk of seeming a hopeless reactionary, I will admit that I am a firm, steadfast believer in him. One has only to scratch the surface of the ancient Greeks, and later the Romans, to realize how uncannily accurate were their cosmic observations. When Zeus appeared, he became the man of destiny, the man who, through luck, pluck, and extraordinary success in warfare, rose to be the ruler of our Earth, and in the process, the heavens too. That, unquestionably, is a pinnacle not attained by lesser warriors and lends credence to his claims.

It is a fact that during his incandescent years of exalted fame, Zeus never forgot his family. He is remembered for putting his brother Poseidon, later called Neptune by the Romans, in charge of the seas, and another brother, Hades, in charge of the nether world. (As assignments go, I have to assume that the nether world, or hell, was the less desirable of the two.) Another brother of Zeus was not honored at all, thus causing speculation that he was the black sheep of the family, or possibly not even Zeus' real brother. Historians may want to further explore this. It is also true that Zeus, before he moved to Mount Olympus, resided on the island of Crete, specifically atop Mount Ida, a noble mountain on that land.

Ida is remembered by Americans today, or was, at least, during the 1920s and 30s, by the song "Ida, Sweet as Apple Cider" which was made popular by the singer Eddie Cantor. I realize that this does not relate directly to my account of Zeus, but I include it here because I believe Americans in their nineties will find it of interest.

Continuing, I have read, but cannot confirm, accounts which claimed that any Greek warrior who laid down his life on behalf of Zeus, went to heaven and was attended day and night by seventy-two vestal virgins. Whether the warrior was permitted unlimited liberties with them is not clear, but it does seem likely. If so, then the "lucky" man might indeed have suffered from creeping debility, leading to eternal ennui. A devastating thought. And were the virgins really vestal?

But again I have digressed. It is important to note that with the passage of time, other religions sprang up like wildflowers in the spring, and that divided the allegiances of religious followers into many splinter groups, sometimes leading to religions *du jour*. (Presbyterians, Methodists, Anglicans, Catholics, Mormons—are just a miniscule few of the solid survivors.) They gradually took over, leaving Zeus at the back of the pack. This was unfortunate and doesn't seem fair, because Zeus was here first, and it is always painful to see a god fall from grace.

Nevertheless, I hold firm to my conviction that Zeus was not just a pretender, but that he was, and still is, the real supreme being of our universe. And I adhere to this even though our great astronomers of today, through the lens of the powerful Hubble telescope, are as yet unsuccessful in their efforts to locate him. But I'm certain they will.

The Boundless Bride

All brides are radiant when they walk down the aisle, but Vanessa Crispy transcended even that definition as she began her measured steps, each strictly in synch with the organist's deliberate rendition of Wagner's "Wedding March." She projected an aura of supreme confidence because she knew that every detail of her wedding had been perfectly planned and would be carried out to her express wishes. She had colored her crinkly brown hair to match her carnelian earrings, and with her crooked little smile and dappled complexion, she stood out like a lighthouse on a rocky shore.

Vanessa had found her man, Captain Fergus Steele, the captain of a cruise ship, a man who was definitely not the average "run of the mill" cruise ship captain. He was virile to a fault, and he wore his epaulets and captain's stripes with unabashed pride. In addition, he carried the ship's daily log on his person, oftentimes democratically urging his passengers to read it and suggest changes. No one could deny that he was a man's man. For example, he would refrain from taking his personal launch from ship to shore, electing instead to swim the distance. Launches were for quiche eating weak-kneed wannabe captains, he steadfastly maintained with a lofty air of disdain.

They were perfectly matched, he for she and she for he. Or so it seemed.

But the vicissitudes of life sometimes thrust a monkey wrench smack into the middle of the most carefully laid plans, and that's exactly what happened here. The unraveling began early in the ceremony when the minister (who was no ugly duckling himself) touched Vanessa's hand, perhaps inadvertently. At that precise moment, an unseen current sizzled between them, galvanizing them into action, or into inaction; it was not clear which. It is known that Vanessa began fumbling with a loose thread in her wedding gown, a diversion, all the while sneaking covert glances at the minister. Then, as the ceremony approached its climax, Vanessa, instead of saying yes to the critical question posed at all weddings, said only, "Maybe."

At that moment pandemonium broke out among the guests, and the minister and Vanessa took advantage of this and fell into each other's arms, sobbing happily. The captain sensed immediately that all was not well between him and his bride to have been, but at the same time, he had to admit that he too felt attracted to the minister.

Vanessa's thoughts, out of necessity, began to churn like an out-of-whack metronome. She was wondering why in the world she had ever wanted to marry the captain. First of all, she couldn't swim, and just being on a water bed made her queasy. She had even rebelled as a child when her parents tried to get her to gargle salt water because of a sore throat. With these flashbacks, she knew for certain that she could not marry the captain. It came from above—she had to marry the minister, and that was all there was to it.

Captain Steele was accustomed to taking charge of difficult situations, and he did so here, revealing in the process an admirable streak of gallantry. With a solution worthy of Solomon, he said that as captain of a ship he could perform marriage ceremonies—could do them in his sleep if he had to—and though his heart was sadly buffeted, as if from a rogue wave, he still had the command of his vessel to console him. So, he reasoned, why shouldn't he go ahead and marry Vanessa to her newfound love, the minister. It was such a sensible idea that all of the wedding guests began cheering and stomping their feet in accordance with this logical way of exchanging a Gordian knot for one of marriage.

The captain then performed what to him was a rather ordinary, perfunctory ceremony, and when it was over, he looked at his watch and declared that he must hurry because it was best for him to swim back to his ship before the tide came in.

It would be nice to say that the wedding couple lived happily ever after. And it might have worked out that way except that when the minister and Vanessa began walking down the aisle as man and wife, Vanessa happened to notice one of the ushers, a large, ruggedly handsome man. He was obviously admiring her bosom. When he looked up, their eyes locked for a moment, and it was like the traditional thunderbolt instilling in them a yearning, a call of the wild that the world does not fully understand but still recognizes and honors.

Vanessa's metronome clicked in again. This time, she questioned why she had agreed to marry the minister in the first place, especially since she was an avowed atheist. Not only that, she knew that she liked to spend Sundays lolling around watching wrestling and hockey. And then she had to admit that she knew absolutely nothing about collection plates. These were considerations that she, incredibly, had not bothered to contemplate beforehand.

She was not quite sure what to do at this point, but she began by relying on her primary attribute: intuitiveness. Suddenly, she crumpled to the floor in a billowing heap of white, hoping the handsome usher would rush over to offer his aid.

It was like magic.

The Bus Station

It was a hot and muggy night, and if the waiting room had any air in it, well it wasn't blowing my way. My bus was due at ten and I had couple of hours or better to sit around and do nothing. Lubbock, Texas, is as good a place as any to do nothing—especially when you're nearly broke—like I was. I just wanted to get out of town and up to Cincinnati where I had a fair shot at getting a driving job for Cargo—a midsize trucking firm. I can drive big rigs or anything—been doing it for thirty years but on my last job I got a few dumb speeding tickets and that got me fired—pronto. Believe me, in this racket your reputation for the good jobs goes two steps in front of you. But here I was in the waiting room with time to spare.

I looked around and decided it looked like any bus station—like a bad day in hell. There were a few pages of an old newspaper on the floor that had probably been walked on a hundred times, but there wasn't anything else to read, and I didn't really care because I don't like to read much anyway. The only other person in the room was some woman—she was facing me and sitting not too far away. She didn't look too good though—maybe she was fifty—I don't know—and her hair was kind of stringy—kind of straggly—uncombed anyway. Besides that, her dress was wrinkled and cheap-looking, and she probably never was too pretty to begin with. Then I thought—what am I thinking?—I'm no handsome dog—I'm older than her—fifty-eight almost, and could use a bath. While I was mulling this over she looked straight at me, and I guess I had been staring at her because our eyes met and then shot off in different directions. So I forgot about her.

It was quiet in the room—all I could hear was a few bugs batting themselves silly against a light bulb and a mosquito that was dive bombing me. That's all I heard. Then I noticed an old birdcage hanging from the ceiling by a rusty chain, and I asked myself—what in a cat's dream would a birdcage be doing here in this place? Its door was open, and if there was ever a bird in it, it was long gone—maybe twenty years. The cage was almost above the woman's head, and while I was thinking about that, our eyes met again. This time I coulda sworn she was wantin' to say something to me—it was just a feeling I had, but unless she was a pro or something like that, I couldn't guess why she'd want to talk to me. Then I felt bad again, thinking she might be a pro or even an ex-pro due to her age. Right then she coughed—a couple times—and that's when she asked me if I had a cigarette. So that was it. My hand sprang to my shirt pocket like it was on a spring and I pulled out a crumpled pack of Camels, and even though there was four or five cigarettes left, I motioned for her to keep the pack. I didn't mean to do that—they were all I had. She put two fingers together and waved a kind of thank you, and then put the pack in a big cloth bag that was on the floor beside her. She didn't even smoke one of them, and I couldn't believe it. Anyway, about twenty minutes went by and then I heard a bus coming into the overhang outside the station—the headlights flashed as it went by and then it stopped—leaving the motor running. I saw that it said Albuquerque—it was heading for Albuquerque. The woman picked up her bag and walked out the door and I saw her get on the bus. She never looked back. I don't know why but I started thinking—it's funny—here's this woman—I never seen her before but now we've seen each other—course nothing happened except for the cigarette thing—but we've seen each other, and then she gets up and heads for Albuquerque, and I'm going the opposite way to Cincinnati. Never in a million years will we see each other again. I don't know why but this made me feel kind of lonely—kind of sad-like—and it didn't make any sense to me. Then I thought it over and I thought yeah, it did make sense, 'cause I knew that this is how things have always been for me—it's been like this for all my life.

Potted Palm and Me

Potted Palm is my best friend and has been for the thirty five years that I've known him. Potted is not his real first name, of course, but Palm is his surname, and our friendship has been ongoing, with little humps and bumps, since we both lusted for the same cute, spindly brunette who sat just ahead of us in our third grade class. The girl, Jackie, liked me at first, and let me walk her home every day. But a month later, Potted was doing the escorting. Shortly after that the little gadabout was being convoyed by a fourth grader who was more worldly and definitely more athletic than either one of us. Potted and I learned a lot about life during the third grade.

Our friendship continued through our early years, and at age eighteen, I enrolled at UCLA, and Potted did the same at USC. We both still lived with our parents, but we would get together whenever we could. One evening, on one such occasion, we had a few beers, more than that actually, and on impulse, we confiscated some half-filled paint cans from my parents' garage. (I swear it was his idea, although he vociferously claims it was mine.)

We began driving, with only a fuzzy, undefined mission in mind, and ended up in Santa Monica where we concentrated on beautifying some small potted ficus trees in front of a row of high-end condos on Ocean Ave. The alerted police, when they caught us, were not as amused as we thought they should have been, and our parents were even less so when they came to bail us out. Everyone agreed that we were too old for that sort of thing, and we promised, encouraged by hefty fines, to improve. By the way, that's when Andy (his real name), became christened Potted by me, and the name stuck with everyone, except his parents.

Potted dropped out of college not long afterward, not because of what happened that night, but because he was somewhat of a free soul who simply decided, as they say, to follow his heart. He got a job as a deckhand on a fishing boat in San Pedro, much to the distress of his parents who were then forced to relegate him to second-tier citizenry in the Palm family hierarchy.

Nevertheless, Potted remained unrepentant and seemed to be singularly happy as far as I could determine. I was more dutiful, if less venturesome, and graduated with a degree in computer science, a field that has been good to me, although I have been saddled with an ongoing feeling of life's mission unaccomplished.

Potted did not remain static in his chosen endeavor. He learned the intricacies of commercial fishing well, and within a few years, he was able to become the skipper of his own boat. There followed several years of fantastic catches of sea bass, tuna, and yellowtail, and his sizeable fortune enabled him to be reinstated to first-class status by his parents.

Then his professional luck turned. The unpredictable currents of the Pacific Ocean changed, causing the fish to disperse and diminish in the coastal waters for some time, and because of this, he nearly lost his boat. Once again his parents moaned that he had not finished college, and in their minds "demoted" him for a second time.

Today, Potted has moved into the relatively more stable import/export business and is doing very well, better than I. But his parents died before he reached his latest pinnacle, and thus, they were not able to continue their evaluations of his roller-coaster life.

Potted saved my life on one occasion. We were swimming in the ocean, off his boat and within sight of Catalina Island, when I became tangled in some fish nets that were left dangling. While trying to free myself, I only tangled myself more, ending up facedown in the water. Potted didn't realize this at first, but when he did, he was quickly at my side, somehow getting me back into the boat and applying CPR. Unfortunately, I had been suffering from recurring bouts of depression during this period, and I, sputtering and spitting out water, berated him for having saved me. He in turn called me an ingrate, an ungrateful bastard, and wouldn't speak to me for a couple of months.

But time healed our breach, and we resumed our friendship after he apologized for calling me an unholy name, knowing I had been mentally down at the time, and I responded by thanking him for being the reason I was still here.

Our personal lives have followed similar patterns in that we have, between us, accounted for five childless marriages, three for him and two for me. All of them were train wrecks. Because of this, our court-approved financial obligations have relegated both of us to be crosstown apartment dwellers. I won't dwell on this any further.

But Potted isn't speaking to me again. He invited me over for dinner last week and said he would be serving his specialty—blackened Louisiana catfish. I must explain that Potted fancies himself as a chef nonpareil (an opinion seconded by him). When we disagreed during dinner as to whether the catfish was blackened or simply charred, even his excellent Johannesburg Riesling couldn't save the evening.

So we are at odds again, but that's only temporary, I'm sure. We'll get back together. A lifelong friendship like ours can't go down for the count just because of a mere bagatelle of a gaffe on my part.

Can it?

And Now for the Kids

I think we all realize how important astrological forecasts are to its adherents and how much they contribute to everyone's health and wellbeing. Although the predictions are always unerringly accurate, no one seems to notice that they apply only to adults, and because of that they are by definition incomplete. Unfortunately, they totally ignore our youngest and most important population—our progeny. I have discovered, after much study and countless celestial calculations that the heavenly bodies contain other configurations that are specifically pertinent only to toddlers ages one to four.

Having ascertained this, here are my forecasts for today:

Aries—Your grandmother is coming to visit, and she is desperate to have you like her. Give her a big hug and a wet kiss, and you will receive gifts as great or greater than those borne by the Three Wise Men.

Taurus—Your argument with your younger brother is disconcerting, but not devastating. Remember that sibling rivalry does not signify the advent of World War III. Perhaps you should relent and let him hug your teddy bear once in a while. There's more. Your cat has been let out of the house. Stay clear of sandbox until further notice.

Gemini—You are intrigued by a picture of an elephant on the wall. This does not prophesy political persuasion. It suggests, instead, an interest in zoology or possibly feng shui.

Cancer—You are alert and show signs of favorable intelligence. You have A, B, and C down pat, but are shaky on D, E, and F. It is too early for you to consider yourself more intellectually endowed than others. Your parents will disagree.

Leo—Your vocal capabilities indicate a hefty range that is ingrained and potent. This enables you to maintain control over your parents and everyone else within two hundred feet. Tonight, vent your lungs to the fullest—for no reason at all—and that will be the ultimate high for you. However, you will hate yourself in the morning.

Virgo—The conjunction of Pluto and Venus indicates that travel is in your horizon. Sorry, but this only means a trip to your pediatrician. He will poke you uncomfortably and make you cry, and then will regain your favor by giving you a Walnetto.

Libra—The stars indicate a change in your life, and it will come soon. Your relief will be immediate, appreciated by you, and even more so by everyone nearby. Brightly colored safety pins become you. See Aquarius.

Scorpio—The stock market appears to be favorable for investing. It is regrettable that you are too young to participate, but be practical and plan ahead. For starters, stop fraternizing with your four-year-old friend who will, one day, be hawking worthless mining stocks and will serve time in jail as a result.

Sagittarius—Your pacifier is wedged between your mattress and sideboards and won't be found until tomorrow. This will frustrate you of course, but don't worry, it will not permanently skewer your psyche. Keep a stiff upper lip (and lower). A new mobile is on the way.

Capricorn—(Girls) You female Capricornians are, without exception, shameless little coquettes. Evidences of flirting are already flaring up and threatening to stampede out of control. (Boys) Get out your Lego, pronto, and pretend total concentration. Be resolute. Resist the siren calls.

Aquarius—Potty training is in the offing for you, probably beginning today. You can resist it, as I'm sure you will, but at the same time be realistic because you will have to give in eventually—unless you are a bird.

Pisces—For some reason there is nothing new in the stars for you today. Anything goes.

Adolph and Eva

The air was dank and sour, but the mood in the bunker was lively because Adolph and Eva had decided on a date and time to be married and it was now. Why not be festive even though above them Berlin was collapsing and the Thousand-Year Reich had been condensed into eleven years. Adolph, ever the optimist, clinked for attention on a champagne glass and proposed a toast saying that the eleven years had been a great experience, and he wouldn't change one iota of it. Everyone applauded and began chanting—eleven more years, eleven more years, an outpouring of faith that clearly humbled Adolph.

Well, marriage trumps all, as the saying goes. At least it was so for Adolph and his pleased-as-punch bride-to-be. (Hermann Goering thoughtfully sent a telegram stressing his regrets for not being able to attend.) A barrel of Lowenbrau had been conveniently lowered by rope into the bunker and was now being freely tapped.

But Adolph and Eva had secretly made plans to escape the bunker, plans that Adolph's lieutenants and assembled guests knew nothing about. As it turned out, the opportunity to pull off the caper came early, right after the ceremony and before the cutting of the cake. A series of *Heil Hitler* salutes had spontaneously begun taking the place of eleven more years. Adolph and Eva, on their hands and knees, took advantage of the canopy of outstretched arms and crawled through an air vent they had cased earlier, making their way to the street above. Eva's white wedding gown was torn and dirtied during the crawl, but they were together and happy. They had pulled off the event of the year. Naturally, they were soon missed by their coterie of well-wishers, and so, the small but tastefully planned reception was necessarily canceled. The guests were somberly perplexed by this sudden end to the festivities, and in addition, they were left with no choice but to go ahead with their previous commitment.

In his late youth, Adolph became proficient at wallpapering. He was quite adept at mixing his paste to just the right consistency, almost never leaving any bubbles in his finished work. It was a labor of love. But when inflation was rampant in Germany and the cost of strudel climbed to two thousand marks, wallpapering was cut from the budget of most people's homes. This forced Adolph to go into politics. At first, in order to draw attention, he would stand on a street corner in Munich, holding a sign that said, "Honk if you love sauerbraten" and then would give a prepared speech. Because of his originality and style the President of Germany, Paul Von Hindenburg, was able to perceive the raw potential in Adolph and was instrumental in promoting his rise to power.

While working their way through the bombed-out streets and buildings of Berlin, Adolph and Eva occasionally stopped to pick up bricks and stones and throw them aside. It was only a gesture, but they wanted to do whatever they could to help in the reconstruction of their beloved city.

What happened to them after this is not entirely clear, details are sparse, but they were apparently able to catch the Deutsche Bahn out of Berlin, a train that took them to Baden-Baden where, before long, they were enjoying the therapeutic aspects of the spas in that historic city. From a honeymoon perspective, though, it was a fizzle because Eva found that while Adolph's spirit was willing, his body was not. It was embarrassing, but she accepted her fate with a minimum of grumbling at the time. However, after Adolph's death she ruefully admitted to a close friend that had she not been so prudish and late in discovery, she almost certainly would have opted for another man.

While in Baden-Baden, they noticed a colorful poster tacked on the wall of their bed and breakfast that extolled the exotic land of Argentina. Wanting to start a new life unencumbered, Adolph called the Baden-Baden International Airport and was fortunate to be able to book two coach seats on a Lufthansa red-eye heading for that land of shining sun and promise.

It was late at night when they arrived at the airport, and almost immediately, a security agent looked suspiciously at Adolph and asked to see his passport. It was a tense moment, but fortunately Adolph had shaved off his mustache and had thought to white-out his name and type in Dr. Christian P. Von Bloomgarten. The agent, who was tired and near the end of his shift, looked at Adolph, then looked at his watch, then looked at the document, then looked at Adolph again, then stamped *APPROVED*.

They were on their way.

The Heil Hitler salute had an inception that is worth noting. Adolph (who came up with the idea early on during an evening at a Munich bier garten) didn't particularly want to instigate it, but he had a fear of germs, and the salute was a good way of avoiding handshaking. On the positive side, the number of colds that Germans had during Adolph's reign was markedly down.

On arrival in Buenos Aires, they were dazzled by the wonderful weather, the world-class cuisine, and the prospect of tango lessons which they had always wanted to pursue but never had the time for due to Adolph's busy schedule. At first, the setting seemed idyllic, but unfortunately, they soon became disenchanted with the city upon discovering that it was overrun with Germans. Adolph complained, saying there were so many of them he couldn't throw a rock without hitting one. (He had been born in Linz, Austria, and didn't particularly like Germans in the first place.)

He also came to dislike his next-door neighbor, an unrepentant communist (and worse, a socialist as well) who was always trying to proselytize him. This kept up until Adolph had his fill, and that came sooner than expected. He and Eva considered moving to Brazil, and the more they thought about it, the better it sounded. So they made preparations to leave, even though this meant the twenty tango lessons they had paid for in advance would be forfeited without refund.

Rio de Janeiro turned out to be a propitious choice for them. It was alive, exciting—even more so than Buenos

Aires—and best of all, there was not a communist, socialist or German to be found. Almost no one was looking for the pair by this time, convinced they had remained in the bunker and perished along with everyone else. But dime store pulp writers kept churning out bestselling books saying: "They're still alive, they're still alive," and even those writers were surprised to learn, much later, that they had been correct all along.

Early in their stay, Adolph resumed wallpaper hanging in order to pay the rent for their Favela shack nestled in the hills above the city. He and Eva would laugh every time he said that wallpaper hanging was better than just plain hanging.

His final days were spent slapping on paste while singing obscure Brazilian folksongs in a confusing German/Portuguese accent—stopping only to feed fresh liver to his adoring Pomeranians, Wienerschnitzel, and Sauerkraut. (He always had a soft spot for dogs.)

The locals found him quaint and enjoyed his imitations of Charlie Chaplin's little tramp. They would laugh when he waddled across the room, wiping excess paste on his pants, and then licking his fingers.

It is not known whether anyone ever recognized him, but if they did, they never came forward, perhaps because there were not many wallpaper hangers in Rio who were his equal.

It is known that he died in Eva's arms at age ninety-one, and that his final poetically inspired words were, "Hand me my pot so that I may stir some paste."

The Great Discovery

A large part of the history of the Goth and Visigoth tribes residing in Europe dating from the second century AD has been, for the most part, well chronicled by historians. But new evidences of their wanderings and behaviors occurred about sixty years ago and have just now come to light. Here is an account that provides the world with information that needs to be known but has not been previously revealed.

The year was 1947 and the month and day were Saturday, June 27. That is the day that Turley Goth made a historic discovery near his hometown of Roswell, New Mexico. His discovery didn't make much of a splash in *The Bugle Call Rag*, Roswell's daily, because a UFO had crash-landed nearby three days before and aliens were known to have survived and infiltrated the area.

Turley, on this hot summer day, was out digging for rare desert truffles, found only in Roswell's nutrient-rich desert sands. It may have been fate's intention for him to stub his big toe on a nearly buried rock, but that didn't stop him from hopping around in circles, sorry he had not worn shoes. But curious by nature, he decided to extract the heavy stone and was dazzled (after a cursory dusting off) by its burnished appearance. He thought he had discovered gold, but when it was later assayed, it turned out to be pyrite or fool's gold, which is known to be near worthless. That did not diminish the importance of his discovery though, because Turley immediately realized that he had found a tablet that possessed inscriptions about an ancient peace-loving people called the Goths.

Turley excitedly began reading the words on the slab, something he could do with modest proficiency because it was written in ancient Sanskrit and that was a language he had studied during his junior year at Warren G. Harding high school in Roswell. (Fortunately, it was a language requirement for graduation at this school.)

"Holy balderdash," Turley blasphemed uncontrollably, as he became engrossed in his find. He immediately raised his eyes to the heavens and apologized for using the word "Holy" in vain. Importantly though, he had just recognized the name of a many times removed cousin of his, Twila Goth. He even rescinded the balderdash when he realized, welling with pride, that this discovery linked him to the famed Goth ancestry. Unfortunately, as was explained on the slab, little was known about Twila, except that she died peacefully in her bed of angel hair straw soon after being bitten by an emotional werewolf.

It should be explained that this is a segment of history that had been, until Turley's discovery, curiously overlooked by historians. The period I am referring to outlines the emergence of the aforementioned Goths who lived on the shores of the Sea of Angelica, near the legendary Pinnacle Plains. During this time, they lived a carefree existence, cavorting, drinking and dancing with abandonment to the insistent beats of their hand-hammered finger cymbals, all the while exhibiting an overt patina of savoir faire.

Life was joyfully unencumbered, and they proliferated shamelessly, never having to go to confession (which was yet to be ordained). Thus, in an astonishing few years, their progeny was swarming all over the Plains, creating what obviously might have been expected—fire alarm bedlam. But the adults, somehow managed to remain manifestly insouciant and oblivious to it all.

Life continued in this idyllic fashion until the death of their patriarch, an esteemed man revered for his profligacy. Unfortunately though, family animosities began to surface during the reading of his will. (Contesting of wills was rather common in those days—not like today.) The main bone of contention was over who would inherit the finger cymbals which were the heart and soul of the now restive community. Unable to resolve their differences, one branch of the Goth family broke off and became known as the Visigoths. (The "Visi" was merely an abbreviation of "Visitation" because the grandparents retained rights to see their grandchildren.)

The result of all this turmoil was that the Visigoths began hyperventilating, breathing what turned out to be faux fire, evolving into cowardly warriors who would fight only when their enemy's back was to the wall. The Goths, a more benign sect, preferred to run instead of fight—not at the first sign of danger—but the second.

The two factions, at loggerheads over their irreconcilable differences, decided to pursue the only sane option ever known to mankind—and that was to declare war. It became widely referred to as the Twenty Years' War of the Finger Cymbals.

Unfortunately, the results of their confrontations remain unclear because the writings on the tablet were dimmed by the ravages of time and were further obliterated by what appeared to be intentional smudges of pomegranate juice.

If that's not enough, future revelations are extremely unlikely because in 1948, one year after the original UFO crash, three aliens broke into Turley's home in Roswell, tied him up and stole his tablet. He was able to see them clearly through his opaque, stained-glass window and watched helplessly as they retreated to their replacement UFO, a sparkling new (vapor-trail-resistant) model. Once inside, the craft slowly rose to about thirty feet aboveground and then disappeared with a whoosh. There has never been a more perfect getaway.

But the jubilant absconders were certain to be in for a shock when they returned to their own planet (coincidently also called Earth), only to learn that their coveted stone was pyrite, as previously mentioned—and only worth about ten dollars, market price.

Final note: Because our own government was clueless regarding any knowledge of UFOs, England's Scotland Yard was called in, and its detectives proved eager and ready to help by offering advice based on their storied reputation. However, in a short while, England called its detectives home, apologetically explaining that their area of expertise was confined to crop circles.

Spreading the Gospel

Mickey Elwin walked into a business office associated with a Muslim mosque and began a conversation with an attractive young lady who was seated behind a desk.

"Hello, my name is Mickey Elwin, and I am interested in joining the Muslim faith. May I speak with someone who can help me?"

"Well, my name is Alama Gardi, and yes, I'll be glad to help you. But if you don't mind, we normally ask a few questions and then follow this up with some instructions and further preparation so that one may gain insight and knowledge of our religion before making a final decision to commit."

"That's very understandable," I said, "So if you have time right now, please feel free to ask me any questions you would like."

"Thank you. I notice by your name and appearance that you are most likely not of Middle Eastern descent. I would like to know where you are from and to learn something of your religious background."

"Of course. I was born and raised in Brawley, California, and my parents and family have always been of the Christian persuasion. So naturally, from birth, I have been the same."

"I see. May I ask why you are dissatisfied with your present religion and wish to renounce it in order to become a Moslem."

"Oh, I'm not unhappy with it at all and have no intention of renouncing it. I just wish to be a Moslem while retaining my belief in Christianity."

"Hmmm. Really? This is highly unusual. In fact, I don't believe I know of anyone who has ever done this. I'm a bit perplexed, and I'm afraid that it will not work out. Are you certain you want to do this? I'm sorry, sir, but I don't believe I can help you after all."

"I was hoping that you could help me. Is there anything in either the Bible or the Koran that says a person can not believe in more than one religion at the same time?"

"Well, not that I know of—at least not in the Koran, but it's just not done. No one ever does that, so again, I'm sorry. If I may, let me make a suggestion to you. There's a Jewish temple less than a mile from here. Why don't you go there and inquire about converting to Judaism?"

"Oh, I've already done that. I am a Jew—have been one for over a year now. I was just recently bar-mitzved.

"Of course, of course, I should have—well, at least you're not an atheist, praise Allah. No, wait—I suppose you're an atheist too."

"Absolutely, one can't be too careful these days."

"I'm beginning to understand. Now please excuse me, Mr. Elwin because I'm behind in my work. If you will leave your name and phone number, I will get back to you when I have time."

"I'll be glad to do that. I don't want to pester you, Ms. Gardi, but I do have one more question. Would you by any chance happen to know where the nearest Buddhist temple is located?"

"Yes I do, and believe me, I'm more than happy to accommodate you. When you go outside, walk to the first signal, turn left, and there's no way you can miss it. Right in front you'll see a statue of the big guy who could never pass up a McDonalds."

"Thanks so much Ms. Gardi, and I'll be waiting to hear from you."

"Stay by your phone, Mr. Elwin. By all means, stay by your phone."

The Heart and Music

It may seem unusual to compare a Cadillac to the human heart and then on to music, but I will try. A Cadillac is by acclaim a very good automobile, and if treated well, has a long life expectancy, perhaps twenty years or more. But keep in mind that it never runs continuously. The human heart, on the other hand, has no lull. While God elected to rest on the seventh day, the heart has to be on watch 24/7. If the possessor has a few good genes (and is lucky) that can be parlayed into a hundred years. So I suggest that the heart is the "real" Cadillac and the car, by comparison, is nothing more than a ho-hum Hyundai.

I realize that what I have said so far is overtly clinical and fails to take into consideration the metaphorical aspects of our most important organ. We like to think of our heart as being the core and essence of our being from which feelings of romance, music, love, and honor emerge. Our poems and songs burst with this message, even to the point of getting a trifle sticky at times. For example, one day a year, we allow ourselves to believe that our hearts are shaped like little red Valentines. ("My Funny Valentine," a great but overworked song, helps to perpetuate this image.)

Leonard Bernstein once said that he believed our penchant for rhythm in music stems from the beating of our hearts. I doubt that. In my opinion our heartbeats are too variable to account for the strict time that our music so often requires. One of the meanings of *ad libitum*, of course, is "freedom from tempo." But whereas our cerebral emotions tolerate a certain amount of "ad lib," before long we natives become restless and then can only be sated by the unwavering insistence of the beat. And the beat goes on. However, going back to Leonard Bernstein, I have to admit that I would accept his opinion over mine, anytime.

But let me cite an example to support my case: A young man's heartbeat may be coasting along at *moderato cantabile* until he sees a pretty girl. At this point, his heart quickly *accelerandos* to *allegro con moto*. If she smiles at him in an encouraging sort of way, it ratchets again into *prestissimo glorioso*. On the other hand, if the girl rejects his overture, his heart slams on the brakes *molto ritardando*, spiraling down to *adagio tristezza*—and his whole day is ruined.

See what I mean?

We're Reeling in the Silk, Baby

Now we live in the Grand Bahamas,
Dressed to the nines in white pajamas,

We're reeling in the silk, Baby.

>Although we are rich, we strive for more . . . using wriggling
>producers that understand not the utility of their efforts.
>>Silk is our
>measure, our treasure . . . at once real and yet illusory.

We enter the market when it hovers low,
and say "Bye bye" when it's high, you know.

That's reeling in the silk, Baby.

>The gossamer threads are delicate . . . and yet so strong . . .
>>perfectly
>designed by nature's programmed providers. Then we
>>bring in the human
>weavers, who, like beavers, work tirelessly at their craft.

Underneath an Asian quilt, soft as silt
We sleep and wake, luxuriate,
With not a whit of guilt.

We've made our mark, Baby.

Maybe!

Only Slightly Askew
(Timeless)

I was in a tube, a tunnel perhaps, and it was clear to me that I was now a goner. This passageway had a pale magenta aura—not white like people who have had near-death experiences seem to describe in most accounts. I was obviously heading somewhere but I didn't know where, and I wasn't anticipating it to be heaven because of my beliefs, or disbeliefs, if you will. And yet I knew that I was ascending, like being in an elevator, except at unbelievable, breathtaking speed.

Now I remembered what it was that caused my dire situation. My wife Poppy and I had been celebrating our fiftieth wedding anniversary at the Dandy Divan Bar and Grille in our hometown, Davenport, Iowa. We and our friends were all in a circle dancing the Jewish Hora when I went into the middle of the group and started showing off, attempting the Kazatzke, the Russian dance where you go down on your haunches, placing your arms in a folded position, while kicking one leg out at a time. I could do that pretty well when I was twenty, but this time it was a major, major mistake. I fell to the floor, not for the first time, but for the last.

It was soon after that I knew I was in the tunnel, and according to my prior beliefs, the chances of there being a heaven or hell were almost nil. If they did exist, I reasoned, I would certainly be a candidate for the lower of the two regions.

A candidate, yes, but that's not the way it turned out. When I alighted, no one could have been more surprised than I. My first awareness was that there was no question about where I was—and did I ever feel sheepish.

I can only say that what I was now experiencing was a feeling—a euphoric consciousness such as I had never felt before. It was a sense of sustained rapture that seemed to pour forth. But even so, I was perplexed as to why I was chosen to be among the chosen. At least I knew that Poppy and I would be reunited someday because she was such a good person, and like all good Catholics, she had been to confession hundreds of times, even when she had to make up things to confess. (I might add that she was also incredibly lucky at bingo.) There was just no doubt that she would join me later.

One of my early surprises was that I was assigned a roommate. This man, who soon became seminal to the course of my future, had already been a person of celebrity while on Earth. He was Jammy Swiggert, a televangelist in former life. He was an ebullient, outgoing fellow (or seemed to be) who loved to demonstrate his friendliness by slapping people on the back. Right away, he did just that to me, so hard it moved one of my vertebrae a tad to the left or right. This was something that would have put me in a brace for a month on Earth, but here it healed instantly, leaving just a twinge. (Obviously one of heaven's perks.)

My afterlife proceeded ecstatically, for a while at least, until Jammy found out that I had been a nonbeliever during my time on Earth. Why, he asked, was I in heaven if I was not called to believe in my prior life? I said I didn't know—I had nothing to do with it. Well, it's not right, he said. You should have been a believer to begin with, so you shouldn't be here now. I am here, I said, and that's all that matters. You need to repent, Jammy said. Why? I said, and on and on it went.

At this point my afterlife degenerated into a figurative hell. Jammy was on my case all of the time. Why me, I wondered. But then, why not me? What else did he have to do all day long? He soon enlisted his friends, some of whom were formerly his hotshot financial supporters and some who were acquaintances from the streets of New Orleans, mostly women, and they all began taunting me, saying I didn't deserve to be here, echoing Jammy who was clearly their spiritual leader.

Fortunately, one thing I learned while in heaven was that anyone could talk to God just by saying, "Please God," providing it wasn't for a frivolous request, like asking for dessert seconds or some such trifle. At any rate, I decided I couldn't take any more bullshit from Jammy and his cronies, so I simply said, "Please God," and my connection went through immediately.

"Hello, God speaking. I'm busy but what can I do for you, Freeman?" (I was so impressed that God, apparently possessing a built-in rolodex, could come up with my name.)

"Thank you for taking my call," I said, trying to gather my thoughts. "First of all I would like to compliment you on your impeccable command of English and I also wish to tell you how wonderful . . ."

"I know, I know, everything is wonderful—but—so get to the point already," God said.

"Right. That's very perceptive," I replied. "Therefore let me quickly say that I would like to have a roommate change. I can't stand Jammy Swiggert anymore."

"You're in heaven aren't you, or am I wrong? You better believe it doesn't get any better than this, my friend."

"You don't know Jammy," I said.

"You're being impertinent," God replied, correctly, and I began to realize that I was in way over my head. Since our conversation was not playing out the way I had hoped, I decided to get down on my knees and resort to groveling, "Please, God, can I have Abraham Lincoln as my roommate instead of Jammy?"

"Absolutely not. Abraham is on level 10."

Now that really stopped me as I stood back up reflexively. I tried to think about what the Bible said about levels and couldn't come up with anything. (But then I had not managed all of the Bible.)

"What level am I on?" I asked, trying to regain my equilibrium. "You are on level 1, Freeman, and you are a very lucky man to be here although you do not seem to realize it."

"Thank you, thank you," I said, trying to sound as sincere as I could. "Then how about moving Jammy Swiggert up to level 2?"

"No televangelist has ever been on level 2," God quickly retorted, His voice rising with irritation, "and stop trying to be so clever. Furthermore, I have given you more call time than you deserve, and I'm telling you right now that you have two choices. You can stay where you are and learn to get along with Jammy or you can go directly to hell."

The response I made just rolled off my tongue, and I immediately knew it was a big, big mistake—even bigger than doing the Kazatzke. I blurted out, "I'll take my chances in hell."

Just before the line went dead, I heard God's fading words, "Don't call me, I'll call . . ."

I was immediately back in a tunnel, and I knew it was a different one because this time it was the color of old coffee grounds. And I was going even faster than in the first one—perhaps because it was all downhill.

My entry into hell was like stepping off an air-conditioned space capsule onto the desert floor of Death Valley on any August 15. There were flames to be sure, but at least they were off to a side and I was not in the middle of them. Simple logic dictates that one could not stand directly in the fire without becoming toast, and therefore no one would make it through the millennium, let alone the millennia. But like anywhere on Earth, one learns to adjust, and that's what I did; at least as best I could.

I might mention that there are no seasons in either heaven or hell, and of course, no one has any reason to wear a watch. But I do recall that Jammy had managed to bring his Rolex with him, and I have to confess that I smuggled in my fake Timex.

With little to do, I began roaming around looking for something of interest just to occupy myself. Before long, I discovered some knobs under some old charcoal briquettes that at first appeared to be burned out but were not. I wondered if they might possibly be controls for the heat. Although they were quite hot, I managed to turn them a notch, and voila!—there was a miniscule lessening of the flames. I expected God to immediately call me to task for this serious infraction, but oddly enough, he didn't. Therefore, on well-spaced occasions I began sauntering back to the knobs making more microscopic turns, and eventually, it began to make a difference.

My discovery of the flame controls and manipulation of them led to a bit of serendipity that will probably sound a bit fanciful to anyone who wasn't there, but here's what happened. Before long, a rough-looking character (and there were many of them here) came up to me and said that Mr. Benjamin Siegal would be deeply honored by my presence. That is the essence of what he said, but I won't repeat the language he used. For a moment, I couldn't place Benjamin Siegal but then I remembered Bugsy Siegal, famous in Las Vegas and Beverly Hills, in fact everywhere, even the Outback. I already knew, thank goodness, that no one called him Bugsy to his face. What happened was that I was escorted rather roughly to where Mr. Siegal was sitting, with his entourage hovering around him.

"I been hearing good things about you being able to take the heat off me," Mr. Siegal said, laughing at his own joke, thus paving the way for his cohorts to laugh uproariously. Right off, I had the feeling he wasn't going to give me the going over that Jammy Swiggert did. "You're okay, kid," he said. (Calling me a kid was a whopper of a euphemism, but

I thanked him and took it as a sign of acceptance.) Strangely enough, this was the beginning of a camaraderie that came at a time when I could use a friend because, as I've said, there were a lot of tough hombres around this place. With Mr. Siegal on my side no one would dare bother me.

One of the things I did that ingratiated me to Benny (he soon asked me to call him that) was to fashion some dice out of charcoal leavings. This took some effort on my part to get the dice squared so they would give proper rolls, and then I put the "eyes" in the dice by using little rounded fingernail clippings.

"Make the dice honest, but not too honest," Benny said with a sense of understood finality, so I made a special pair for him to use when he was rolling. (You do things like this for a friend.)

We began having some roaring good times with nonstop crap games that attracted quite a few Runyonesque characters—some of whom I found to be more entertaining and colorful than bad. I was beginning to doubt that God always put the right people in hell. Benny had a lot of influence, and I don't know how he did it, but he even managed to have a supply of marshmallows brought in so that we could roast them and party while laying our bets.

The crap games that ensued could not continue unnoticed forever, of course, and as it turned out, they ended sooner than later. I don't know why, but God contacted not Benny but me. I have to admit I was the instigator. He was furious.

"You are a first-class pain in the netherworld, Freeman (those were his exact words and I was shocked), and furthermore, you are making a mockery of the level of loyalty and unfettered moral integrity that I expect of everyone in my jurisdiction, and my jurisdiction is, of course, everywhere, and that by definition includes you in case you don't know it." (I was hoping God would rephrase that last sentence.) Instead, he continued, "Therefore, because of your baldly errant and miscreant misbehavior, I have decided a change in locale is necessary for you so that I can continue my work unimpeded by your discombobulating distractions." Now that really sobered me (not only by his syntax), and I began shaking uncontrollably, fearing that hell, like heaven, might have ten levels, and I'd be headed for the basement.

"I run a tight ship here, and I don't have time for a troublemaker like you," God still kept on, not even pausing for breath, "and don't think I'm not aware of your fiddling with the furnace controls—but because I'm busy bringing in a passel of people from all over the universe, and because I have to decide whether to send each and every one of them up or down, and because of a monumental migraine that you have both triggered and exacerbated I am left with no choice but to send you back to earth for now. Mark my words, though, you'll be back and next time around there'll be no roasting of marshmallows—that loophole has been plugged."

I was flabbergasted and thrilled to know I would be going home, but before I could feign displeasure over his decision our line began to fade and I could hear him muttering, "I really didn't need this,"—followed by a faint click.

I was soon back in the tube and too nervous with excitement to even notice its color. All that mattered was that I was on the express headed back to terra firma where I would be reunited with my beloved Poppy.

It was a hot summer day when I returned, almost a hundred degrees, but I still began to shiver, needing time to adjust to the lower temperature. My reentry surprised me (I was always being surprised, it seems) because I expected to be released at my home, but once again things didn't turn out the way I anticipated. I just stood for a while trying to get my bearings and that's when I noticed a carved wooden sign posted on the lawn of an old, large home. The sign said:

THE SUNNY SIDE
SLEEP INN FOR SENIORS

It finally dawned on me that Poppy might be in a retirement home and maybe this was it. Upon entering the "Inn," a lady at the desk confirmed my inquiry, telling me I would find Poppy in the living area watching television.

I peeked into the room and saw her sitting with about ten other people, all in a row, vaguely watching a large fuzzy, unattended TV screen. She looked beautiful to me, just as she looked when I last saw her. I walked over to her and called her name and when she looked up it was as if she were seeing a ghost incarnate. This was understandable and I sat down in an empty chair beside her, assuring her that I was really back and would explain everything later. We both cried with joy, as we hugged and kissed.

I finally said to her, "Come on, Poppy, let's get out of here. I'm taking you home." She replied, "Well, Free, there's something I have to tell you—I have a little problem."

"Problem? What's the little problem, Poppy?"

"Well, in addition to having sold our home, it's Hubert," she said. This made me nervous, I guess, because I blurted out, "Hubert? Hubert who? Who's Hubert?" With that, she just nodded toward a man seated in a wheelchair on the other side of her. "That's Hubert," she said. "I thought you were gone forever, so I married Hubert—you understand—it was just for companionship." I was not surprised this time, stunned is the word. I had not even noticed Hubert, but there he was, a thin, little wisp of a man with just one strand of white hair on his head, and it was perfectly combed—almost into a spit curl. He had to be at least five years older than I was when I first died. When Hubert heard his name (after it was mentioned for the fifth time), he stirred, looked over at me, smiled wanly, and raised a trembling hand in an effort to shake mine. But the effort was too much for him, and his hand fell limply back onto his wheelchair arm.

And I could tell right then and there that Hubert wasn't going to be a problem.

Pyramids
(Questions without Answers)
True Story

About ten years ago, my wife Angela and I were in Taos, New Mexico, vacationing for a few days. On one of the days, I set out alone on a hike through the cactus and creosote that flourish in the high desert. I happened to notice ahead of me a large mound about eighteen inches high that was composed of tiny pebbles. I was fascinated by it and stopped to observe it. Soon after that discovery, I noticed several more. They appeared to be anthills of gigantic size, and upon closer examination of one of them, I was able to verify this as I could see some rather large ants that were systematically working on their formidable creation. The mound must have been, to the ants, the equivalent in size of an Egyptian pyramid to a human. Perhaps larger.

I then noticed that the ants laboring on their "pyramid" were emerging from a small hole at ground level and they were carrying pebbles, transporting them one by one to the top of the heap. They were in a continual building process, and at the same time were, without doubt, creating (what for them) was a cavernous area underground.

With time to spare and my curiosity aroused, I decided to follow one ant as it arose from the hole. This particular ant was grasping a pebble that was probably several times its size and weight. It exited from the hole carrying its "huge rock" and began to ascend the steep incline, a predictably formidable task. On the way up it, at times, slipped backward and downward, then regained its footing and once again worked its way upward. Occasionally, the ant dropped the pebble, then retrieved it and continued as before. When it finally reached the summit, it deposited the pebble and then, its duty done, began the downward trek. Upon reaching the base, the ant reentered the original hole, presumably to repeat the process. The entire procedure took about twenty minutes.

We know that ants have brains, but they are so infinitesimal that their body of cells possess, perhaps, something comparable to a minimal computer chip—a component that programs and instructs them. But their mounds, at least to our human level of reasoning, make no sense. They are not constructed in meaningful contexts, and the pebbles could have more easily been spread anywhere on the desert floor.

The Egyptian pyramids, by comparison and contrast, are architectural wonders; each stone honed to exact size and placed with precision into its prescribed slot. The religious significance, of paramount importance at the time, was predicated on the belief that the Egyptian kings (possessing a conceit to support their presumption) were the sons of deities. However, the religion of that time is no longer relevant in modern Egypt or the rest of the world. Thus, aside from housing their own caverns for the deceased kings and providing monoliths that people of today admire in awe, much of the original purpose of the pyramids is negated or at least diminished.

But what do the ants believe? Or, if they believe nothing, as is almost certainly the case, why do they build their "pyramids?"

La Ronde

I live in Highland Park, which, I admit, is not considered to be the toniest section of Los Angeles. In fact, the area where I live may not even be the toniest section of Highland Park, if there is such a section. But I love my home, and, modest though it may be, it's large enough for me and my cat, Gigi.

I only mention this because of what happened a couple of years ago. At that time, I decided to have my *chateau* painted and the color I chose was heliotrope. Heliotrope happens to be my favorite color, with its light tint of purple and reddish lavender cast. My neighbor, Claudette, who emigrated from France by way of New York, likes it too; she even raves about it. She says that even though the color is wickedly *outré* and *extrémement facile* as well, it still has a lilt, a charm within, a *joie de vivre* and a *genre* all its own. Those are her words. I love her command of French and her cute accent, which has a touch of the Bronx in the mix.

Desmond, my best friend, is the man who painted my house, and house painting is his trade. But he doesn't work in Highland Park; not usually, anyway. In fact, he has a devoted clientele in Bel Air who provide enough work for him so that there is a waiting list for his services. Desmond is not of French descent but he addresses his clients as *M'seur* and *M'dame* and that demonstrably elevates him in their minds. Of course, his demand and prices increase accordingly.

But here's what happened. After Desmond painted my home, he began suggesting the same color, heliotrope, to some of his clients, and to his and my surprise, it caught on. It soon became the rage, the "in" color. And it continued to grow in popularity until most of the homes in Bel Air were painted "my" heliotrope. At first, this made me feel so *de rigueur*, so *du jour*, even though I live across town, across the tracks, if you will. I thought these feelings would last a long time. But *au contraire*. My euphoria was destined to be short-lived.

The problem was that heliotrope, as though possessing gigantic tentacles, began to spread insidiously into the hopelessly *gauche* San Fernando Valley. While the inhabitants of Bel Air naturally felt that they alone possessed taste that was truly *distingue*, their inherited sense of *noblesse oblige* obligated them to tolerate the Valleyites and their "take-over," albeit with evidences of understandable disdain. At the same time, the Bel Airians (who do not openly discuss money) had to face reality and feared that the theft of "their" color would cause real estate prices in their fiefdom to plummet. Because of this they gathered and, *tout de suite*, chose a replacement color which could not be readily copied. Their choice was a new color developed by Desmond especially for them, one they believed would remain inaccessible to the Valleyites. It was called *Chocolatte Soiree*. But the Valleyites were not to be denied, and before long—*voila!*—black market vats of *Chocolatte Soiree* were finding their way over the Santa

Monica Mountains and the use of it soon spread like weeds in a verdant vegetable garden.

Today, Desmond is busier than ever, but the bottom line is that my heliotrope is no longer *tres chic*. Because of this, he has suggested that I make a color change, fearing my house is becoming a wretched embarrassment.

"I got you into this mess, *mon ami*," he says, "but I can get you out of it. I'll repaint your house free, except of course for the cost of the paint. Your present color is, how can I say it, so *fin de siecle*. In other words, man, it's definitely down the *Seine*."

But I'm resisting my friend's entreaties. I'm not fickle and I won't bend with a *mistral* unless it becomes a category five. I think I'll just hang on and wait for heliotrope to become fashionable again.

La Ronde.

Designing and Manufacturing

Things are decidedly cheery for me these days. My business is flourishing, and I am considered to have the very best products in my field, a field that I will describe later. But I don't think anyone that I know would ever have dreamed I'd be where I am today considering how I started out.

As a kid I was a real pain in the arse—to my parents, to everyone. In fact, I was thrown out of my home at age eleven, incorrigible, my parents said, and believe me, it was really hard surviving alone in London at that age. But I met my needs and made life bearable by shoplifting, begging, lying; those things and more. Thank the good Lord I never got caught once, at least as a kid.

My downfall, though, came as an adult when I belonged to a gang of highwaymen; okay, common road thieves. Our group was led by an amiable man (ha!) named Casper Winslow. Casper was no Robin Hood, that's for sure. Frankly, he didn't give a fig whether his victims were healthy and wealthy or sick and down to their last shilling. He had mouths to feed, his and ours, mostly his, and that's all that mattered to him.

My association with him and the gang came to a sudden end on a moonless, overcast night when we were working a road in the Warwick area. I was bored stiff as well as numb with cold and no carriages or anything else went by to liven things up. I never saw anyone approaching, but all of a sudden, I was grabbed by two men who I guessed were constables from Warwick castle. (This was confirmed later.) At any rate, I was hauled off to the castle and thrown into a cell that had run out of heat long before I got there. It was just my luck to be the only one of my gang to get nabbed, and I remember the date like it was tattooed on my brain, December 16, 1599.

After a couple of days of reasonably pleasant relaxation but very poor diet, two breathtakingly large gentlemen came into my cell and began pummeling me while simultaneously demanding to know the name of the leader of my gang. Between thumpings, I tried to explain that honor forbade me to reveal my leader's name. I could never do that, I said, and I was sure they would understand my devoted and unwavering sentiments. At first, I thought they did because the pounding suddenly stopped. Instead, without any explanation to me, an alternative had occurred to them, and they hauled me into another room that was no warmer than the first. That's when I saw the rack and right then I knew I was in for it.

What happened is that they tied me with ropes to the rack with my arms and legs splayed out, and I could tell that the cranking of the machine was ready to commence. But right at that moment, even before my body's realignment began, I looked at the rack, sized it up quickly, and realized that there were deficiencies in its design. I could see that its levers and pulleys were not synchronized properly and that the maximum effective ratios could not be attained without much needed changes and revisions. I don't know how I did this, but it was then that I became instantly aware of my natural inclination for mathematical and mechanical reasoning. Still, I had no inkling that this was to become my life's endeavor. For some reason though, I made it a point to store every facet of that rack's design into my head.

The crank began turning and the rack was creaking, and before long, it was ratcheted up a couple of notches. That's when I (unintentionally, I swear) yelled out two bloody words, Casper Winslow. With that, the ungainly machine came to a halt, because, fortunately, that was all the gentlemen wanted of me. Then they, without ceremony and with a distinct lack of finesse, escorted me outside the castle and flung me willy-nilly into a pile of fresh cow chips. At least the chips were soft and relatively warm.

My first reaction on being freed was to feel like my arms were a bit longer than they had been, and I wasn't quite sure if there would be any permanence from this experience or not. Now this may sound strange, but my second reaction was to begin thinking seriously about working on ideas for improving the rack. In fact, that was to become an obsession of mine, and as a result, it has led me to where I am today.

It took me almost a full year of concentrated testing and development before I finally came up with a design that I considered to be a dilly. Of course, I had a lot of assistance along the way. I became friends with a gaoler at Warwick of all places. He provided me, for a pittance, with a steady supply of prisoners whose help I needed to successfully conduct my rigid, high quality tests. They aided me immensely. Having said that, I do feel sorry for those poor chaps who were forced to readily sacrifice themselves on my behalf; first of all, for the tedious hours demanded of them, and secondly, for the rigorous and unexpected stretching they had to endure. I will say this, I believe a few of them were crybabies who tended to exaggerate their lot, and when I found that to be the case, I usually gave them an extra crank or two just to let them know they couldn't fool me. But the bottom line is that in the process, my rack became the world's best, and it has been my most important contribution to humanity.

My business is flourishing today and has been since I first put the rack, my version, on the market. Without question Old Bailey is my best customer, but there's a castle sitting atop every molehill in England, and because of this, I have a backlog of gaols waiting impatiently for my services.

Fortunately, I have a restless mind, so in recent years, I have expanded my business, inventing other quality merchandise such as head vises, thumb screws, pliers, and other products which are necessary adjuncts to my field. They are moneymakers to be sure, and I am doing better than well, but the rack will always be my baby, my pride, and joy.

And I don't foresee any downturn in demand for my services as long as there are good, kindly, conscientious people out there who will do whatever needs to be done in their noble efforts to elicit the truth.

Broadway Brahma

I'm a Brahma bull and I'm damned proud of it. I can guarantee you there's nothing better or higher in the scale of life than the Bovine family. We're the best looking, the smartest and the best adjusted of all the animals—and believe me, the Brahmas are at the top of the heap. I can't rate human beings because they just don't come close enough to our level to be measured.

I live in the foothills outside of Paso Robles, pasturing around gnarled oak trees that overlook the Pacific Ocean. On warm spring days, I can smell the lupine, walk on a carpet of yellow mustard grass, and watch the poppies popping up all over. Life is good.

I don't mean to claim that everything is always perfect here. I can remember, in my youth, when two cowboys roped me to the ground, tied me up, and then branded me. I hadn't done a thing wrong. I wasn't going nowhere, and I certainly didn't deserve it. But even today, it embarrasses me to admit that I bawled like a baby at the time. I still dream at night of being able to put a poker in the fire, get it sizzling hot, and then return the compliment to those bozos who did it to me.

I liked rodeo because I was a star, the best—they called me Broadway Brahma, and the pretty heifers were always bunched together waiting, gorgeous groupies waiting for me when the show ended.

I traveled the rodeo circuit until I developed a touch of tendinitis in my right hind leg, and because of that, I was put out to pasture, no pun intended. That proved to be a blessing though, because my prowess for reproduction soon became legend for miles around. Today. I have so many offspring I can't remember all their names. Every autumn I go to the county fair and pick up a few more blue ribbons, testimony to my procreational exploits. (Who needs opposable thumbs?) As I've indicated, life is good. Sure, there are also times when it's cold and we'll have several days of stormy weather. But when it's like that, I just hunker down under an oak tree and spend my time thinking about all the pretty heifers, lying out there waiting, waiting for the sun and me to come out.

Speaking of heifers, a few years back when I was doing rodeo, my job was to charge out of a gated area with a rider on my back. I would snort, twist, and turn, put on a demonstration, and then throw those guys to the ground—every time. It's hard to believe, but as soon as those idiots healed, they would come right back and do it again. Yes, I put on quite a show.

Just recently, one of my sons (can't think of his name) and I were standing on a small hill overlooking a pasture, and there were about ten or fifteen young heifers lolling around, just waiting for something interesting to happen. They were achingly beautiful—every one of them a Hollywood starlet in my eyes.

My son said, "Come on, Dad, let's run down there and get us one of them heifers." (My son is eager—a chip off the old block.)

I said to him, "No, son, let's walk down and get them all."

Verbalherbal

It is common knowledge that women have longer life spans than men. This is beyond dispute, but the explanation for this has always baffled gerontologists and the scientific community in general.

Several years ago, I became intrigued by the age differential of men and women, and that's when I began to research the causes of this phenomenon. Only recently have I discovered the answer, and its simplicity has surprised everyone, including me. The answer is lungs! Women have larger and healthier lungs than men and in this brief treatise I will explain why this is so.

From the time men are boys, they believe they are the stronger of the sexes; more herculean; better endowed to conquer the physical demands of a challenging world. This happens to be true while they are young, but somewhere around age fifty, the graphs following the courses of life spans begin calibrating up for women and down for men. It is possible this is compensation to women because of the somewhat disconcerting and demeaning fact that they were created from Adam's rib.

But here, in essence, is what really happens. Men, in their middle age, become lung potatoes. Whether by choice or through genetic makeup, they become passive listeners instead of passionate talkers. They contribute to conversations with their wives by saying, uh-huh, yup and yo. Thus, men's lungs, due to lack of usage, progressively diminish in size, severely limiting their ability to expand and contract in a normal fashion without tiring.

Meanwhile, the opposite is taking place with women. They are increasing their lung capacity through the beneficial vibrations of verbal dialogue (use it or lose it). Early on, they do what may at first seem insignificant, like to say to their kids: "Jimmy, you get in the house this instant—be sure to wear a jacket—eat all of your okra or no dessert—your shoes are dirty and you're tracking the floor." It never occurs to men to say things like that to their kids. They just read the paper and occasionally grunt.

It should be pointed out that telephones have become significant contributors to the lung discrepancy, and since the advent of cell phones, the problem has been ballooning exponentially. Everyone knows that when a man goes to the phone, he completes his call in one minute or less while a woman will talk for forty minutes or more before saying goodbye—and then adds five more for good measure. What everyone has been slow to realize is that this same call has expanded the woman's lungs enough to increase her life expectancy by three seconds. Add these seconds together over several generations and you can see where I'm heading with this.

So men are, without question, more verbally deficient than women. To counteract this, they primordially gravitate to their favored emporium and order a brew, believing that, as they sit and muse about their next fishing trip, the brew will keep their lungs rested and moist. It does, but what they don't realize is that they are actually consigning themselves to an earlier grave than women despite the fact that the malt in the beer contains healthy additives.

Unfortunately, most men are still unaware of the disastrous ramifications of lung discrepancy, and so it is difficult to foresee an early resolution to the problem. However, there is some good news. An over-the-counter product called *Verbalherbal* was recently put on the market, and it has proven to be phenomenally successful in increasing male volubility by ten to twelve percent. The only known side-effect is that it tends to cause a reduction in sexual potency. (There are some reports that most women herald this sexual passiveness in their men as a godsend, but that is neither proven nor the thrust of this report.)

Balancing the positive against the negative, *Verbalherbal* may be the key to men's living a longer, if less uplifting life. Think about it, men, and decide for yourselves.

Micaela (Mia)

Nathan Banks was born into a family of wealth, and at a very early age he exhibited obvious signs of mental acuity. By the age of three he was forming his alphabet blocks into words without help or direction of his parents. He also possessed a memory for numbers that astounded everyone. If that were not enough, by the time he entered grade school he had many friends—providing him the added advantage of being a well-rounded boy, as well as one who appeared destained to make his mark in the world.

Continuing on this predictable path, at age sixteen he entered Columbia University, his father's alma mater, and graduated at nineteen, with honors.

That was then.

Nathan is dying. He knows he is dying and he is determined to exit this world in a manner of his own choosing—alone. He will not, as he puts it, languish in a hospital with tubes poked into every orifice of his body. Because his children shun him and he has no wife by his side, he will remain in his home, a voluntary recluse, until he is called upward or downward.

Nathan's four marriages all ended in divorce and each lasted a shorter time than the previous one. It seemed odd to him, as it would to almost anyone, that he couldn't remember what three of his wives looked like—and the fourth, whom he remembered but felt no remorse for, died by her own hand soon after their divorce.

What he did have imprinted on his mind, and would retain to his last breath, was his remembrance of the only true love of his life. Her name was Micaela, or Mia, as his diminutive term of endearment for her was to become.

Nathan, with great effort, leaves his bed. He walks to a picture window and looks at his pool and then to the ocean. His residence is not an ordinary home—it is a mansion.

After his graduation from Columbia, and still not of voting age, Nathan moved to Chicago, accepting an offer to join a firm that dealt in commodities, buying and selling everything from grains to precious metals and beyond. It was, in the beginning, a fortuitous move because it resulted in the first of his expanding fortunes. He was elevated quickly from the floor of the exchange to the literal and figurative upper levels of influence. But at age twenty-five, he suffered an emotional and mental breakdown, the consequence of around the clock concentration on the very work for which he exhibited an exceptional talent. His decision then (and urged by his doctors) was to take a leave of absence for six months in order to regain his health.

He elected to go to Mexico since he had studied Spanish in college and also because he had a great empathy for and appreciation of Mexican people and their culture. He traveled by train, boarding at Mexicali, heading south toward

Guadalajara. A wrong coupling, at first unbeknownst by him, put him on another train that took him to Tampico on the Gulf Coast. He didn't care. From there, he began walking north along the shoreline until he came to a small village that was located at the foot of rounded hills. It was positioned on a rocky promontory with sandy beaches situated below. He looked at this quiet little village and decided to stay there. The village was called Tepic.

Nathan, for all his brilliance, remains obdurate, unable to fathom why every one of his personal relationships failed miserably, leaving him in this untenable situation.

He stayed in Tepic for almost four months, nurturing his idleness while gradually feeling better than he could ever recall. His days were spent diving for conch shells and crayfish, eating the crayfish, and cleaning and keeping the conchs because of their beauty and aesthetic appeal. He sold some of them, for a pittance.

During his second month, while walking on the beach, he became aware of a young Mexican girl approaching him. His first reaction was to wonder why he had not seen this enchanting girl before. She was like an apparition, perhaps occasioned by the tropical sun, he thought. He was impressed by her cool appearance and her confident gait, with her simple cotton dress creasing against her body according to the various directions of the wind from the sea.

As they passed, he said hello to her and she, in turn, averted her eyes but said something softly. At that moment, they both felt an invisible current that arced from one to the other. It was the natural lure of man and woman. He turned to look at her as she walked away but she did not look back.

Nathan lies in his bed, breathing irregularly. He reaches for a Lorcet, a pain alleviator, and swallows it with water. Then takes another and another. Then he, with difficulty, opens a fresh pack of cigarettes and lights one. The cigarette does not taste good, but he smokes it anyway. He has learned nothing.

Two weeks were to elapse before Nathan and the girl were to see each other again. This time, they stopped and exchanged a few words, and that is when he learned her name, Micaela. She seemed pleased that Nathan could speak Spanish, but all too soon, she said that she had to leave in order to go to her father's fishing boat.

Nathan was determined to get to know her. He learned from local people that she was eighteen and the daughter of a local fisherman. Though Nathan was twenty-five, he did not feel that the age difference was significant.

They did meet again along the same strand of beach as before, and this time, Nathan called her Mia. He took her by the hand and they began walking. Mia's shyness disappeared and was replaced by huge smiles, an aurora borealis, Nathan called it. They approached a rocky cove that was obscured by high, craggy rocks, revealing a small beach with turquoise waters lapping against the sandy shore. They were alone for the first time. Wordlessly, they held each other close, and this was followed by kisses that could not be controlled or stopped.

From this time on, they shared a silent, unspoken commitment. But by their actions, their fate was also sealed.

Nathan has no photograph of Mia but he does not need one. He has every facet of her face, every curve of her body, etched in his mind and heart.

It was not long before Nathan met her parents. Micaela's father was a lifelong fisherman as his forbears had been. But her father did not like Nathan. He said he was not Catholic, and he could not fish; therefore, he would never amount to anything. On the other hand, Mia's mother did like him. She wanted to cook for him, and did. She would prepare *ropa vieja* and wrap it in tortillas for him to take back to the shack where he lived. She knew that her daughter was in love with Nathan, and she liked him. As mothers do, she gave her daughter advice while her father was wary, determined to protect her honor.

When her father's fishing boat returned from the sea each day, Mia was always there to meet it. She would oversee the weighing of the day's catch, figuring the value according to the pounds recorded, calculating it with the always-changing market value. Then, she would pay her father's crew their wages earned. Mia's father could not do this, and when Nathan watched her, he was very pleased with the quickness of her mind, because he knew that she had had very little schooling.

With effort, Nathan tries to get out of bed. Instead, he reaches for and then swallows another Lorcet, extra strength, then another. Too much. But what does it matter now?

Nathan and Mia were now completely absorbed in their love for each other, and he wanted her to go to Chicago with him, as he knew he could not stay in Tepic forever. But Mia cried and said that as great as was her love for him, she was needed in the village by her family and she could not forsake them. She pleaded with him to stay.

It was during these conversations that everything was irrevocably decided for the star-crossed couple. Mia's father learned of the affair they were having, and he immediately confronted Nathan, giving him a rapiered ultimatum : "You will leave Tepic by sundown or you will die." Nathan implored her father to understand the deepness, the magnitude of his love for Mia, but her father's emotions were rigid, not to be swayed by a stranger of another culture.

Left without options, Nathan returned to Chicago and plunged again into his natural domain, the world of business. He prospered, and his ability to navigate through difficult financial transactions, along with the honing of his instinct to go for the jugular when necessary, became legend.

He began his succession of marriages and fathered three children, but evidenced no inclination for being either a loyal husband or a good father. He hardly knew, or even wanted to know, his children. Always, in his mind, only Micaela was by his side, putting her smooth brown arms around him—smiling.

Despite the monetary largesse accorded his ex-wives (and he came to know their respective lawyers better than he knew them), he became extremely wealthy, acquired a huge estate in Coral Gables and enjoyed it not at all. His satisfactions in life, his reasons to live, had been stillborn long before.

With a blaze of alertness, Nathan thinks of Mia and tries to sound her name—one last time—but fails. Moments later, the longings, torments, and failings that had scarred his life—cease. He was forty-three years old.

It was now time for the contesters of the Nathan Banks estate to emerge from their dens of waiting, and they did emerge, en masse.

"Toni"

Most everyone realizes how supportive France was of the American colonists during the Revolutionary War, but not everyone knows the attribution of this support stemmed from France's intense dislike of Great Britain. Perhaps the presentation of some of the lesser-known footnotes of history will aid in our understanding of the reasons for their dissension and, in turn, can offer insight as to how much they helped the colonies achieve their independence.

When it came to France's attitude toward Great Britain, there wasn't much of anything to be said in its favor. For example, the French fumed at the name of the channel separating them, the English Channel. They were adamant in their belief that it should have been called the French Channel in the first place. They claimed it was so narrow that the British, who had superior telescopes, could spy on the French ladies—right into their bedrooms. Frenchmen were outraged by this because they were helpless—left without a way to even the playing field.

The French, however, knew they were always superior to the British when it came to culinary achievements. This can be traced to Louis X in the latter part of the sixteenth century. The king's true love was cooking, and he was famed throughout the land for his "Parfait flambe." That was his masterpiece. But the British could never forgive him, because he had written into children's textbooks that anyone who ate Yorkshire pudding would get rickets and their growth would be stunted.

The list of irritations between the two countries was long and unrelenting, and France's disdain for the British was fermented even further when it was revealed that the British preferred warm beer to their unsurpassed wines.

So when it came time to offer aid to the colonies, the French government responded by doing all it could to help the Americans win their bid for freedom. In order to achieve these desires, France showered America with munitions, ships, uniforms, the Statue of Liberty, girls, and barrels of Lafite Rothschild 66. Everything. Great Britain then knew it didn't stand a chance of subduing the colonists once they had received this cornucopia of arms and favors.

Marie Antoinette, in particular, loathed the British. In fact, she was famous for having once uttered, "Let them eat scones." The French people were amused by her demeaning little joke, but when she, curiously, changed scones to croissants and used it on her own people, they were quick to anger. Thus the fickle public turned against her, and their intense reactions were not to be reversed. (Most historians believe she said "Let them eat cake," but that's just not true—and when you think about it, croissants makes a lot more sense.)

It's a shame that this one little mistake became the *raison d'etre* for her instant demise. Until then she was considered to be a very fine, respected lady, beloved by all; one who had even democratically encouraged her subjects to call her "Toni."

The Craven Image Publishing House

Dear Mr. Helmsly,

We, at Craven Image Publishing House, wish to thank you for your interest in our firm and especially for giving us the opportunity to read and review your manuscript for possible publication.

Now, referring to the contents of your writing—we have to admit that we are somewhat baffled by its title, *Such a Lovely War*. It is without doubt an excellent title, but what baffles us most is that you hardly mention war at all in your book, : you only concentrate on peace---with everyone getting along famously. Curious. As you must be aware, stories of war have significantly greater sales potential than those of peace. Even minor skirmishes pique the interest of most readers, but peace is so placid, so jejune, if you will. If you do not wish to stress war, I would suggest that you consider adding some chapters involving intrigue, sensuality, and infidelity; perhaps a dollop of avarice, and of course, don't forget the plague. This would certainly contribute toward enlarging your potential audience, and I believe it could be achieved without lessening the artistic merit of your work.

Having said that, we have some wonderful news for you. We do feel that your book has an abundance of redeeming qualities, and our review staff is diligently striving to define them. I also want you to know that everyone in our office has read your manuscript. It has been passed around many times, and the audible merriment it elicits from one and all has been undimmed by repetition.

Now, before you misconstrue what I am saying, let me elucidate because I have an important point to make. I believe that there is an audience even in such disparate locations such as the Outback, the Steppes, and Barstow, waiting and eager for books that are intended to be serious but in reality bring a smile to the lips of its readers. It is a special gift for writing that few possess. But your book, by having fulfilled these essentials, is a jewel, and you, my good man, are among those especially endowed. At present, you are the best writer I know of in this genre, and while you may not realize it, you are teetering on the cutting edge of a market that has long been waiting to be mined.

A contract should soon be on the way, Mr. Helmsly, but please don't contact us, let us contact you. Meanwhile, just keep plugging and don't give up the ship.

Yours truly,

Chester Craven

Chester Craven, Editor and Publisher

The Agnostisades

I find it of interest that so many people are unaware of the Agnostisades, the conflicts between the agnostics and the atheists that roiled the lives of so many in medieval Europe during the ninth and tenth centuries AD. This antedates the Crusades which were later conducted by the Christians who had God on their side and the Muslims who had Allah on their side. The agnostics and atheists, of course, had no deity or other support group behind them. They were on their own.

During the above mentioned centuries, the agnostics and the atheists were at loggerheads over the issue of whether there was no God, as the atheists insisted, or whether there might be a God but there was no proof, as the agnostics maintained. This latter position greatly agitated the atheists, fueling resentments that erupted into continuous verbal abuses of the agnostics in the form of unmuted oaths, raspberries, and other manifestations of rude, unacceptable behavior.

For a hundred years, there were no martial outbreaks between the two groups, but the atheists during this period, taunted the agnostics mercilessly by assuming a superior attitude, claiming that they were smarter than the agnostics because they were positive there was no God. When they were feeling especially vituperative, they called them "doubting Thomases," a slur directed against Tor Thomas, the titular ruler of the agnostics.

The agnostics became more and more resentful of the second-class status that they were (rightfully or wrongfully) consigned, and they finally decided that the perpetrators had gone too far and they weren't going to take it anymore. The idea of conducting an agnostisade (an unholy war) was presented by Tor Thomas to his followers, and they, tired of being harassed, approved it immediately. "Huzzah, Huzzah, Huzzah," they shouted. (That expression was a bit antiquated, even then.)

The agnostics were stirred to a frenzy, and a call to arms became the hue and cry. Thousands of tracts were printed and tacked to their doors before it was realized that none of them could read or write. Fortunately, they were adept at getting news through the grapevine, a conduit that was honed by their years of worldwide acclaim for winemaking.

The agnostic army was hastily formed and was soon ready to go into battle. The men were exhorted to a fever pitch by shouting Tor's catchy slogan, "Skewer the atheist bastards." The atheists, of course, recognized the negativity of this, and they in turn assembled their own army in order to defend themselves against the inevitable onslaught.

The conflict between the two armies began on the jagged hills and rutted gullies of Poland on July 4, 819. For a while, it progressed rather evenly, first one side prevailing and then the other. But the toll on both sides began to mount as thousands of "nonbelievers," as well as the "show-me-the-proof" adherents fell, smote by lances, pikes, rapiers, and other state-of-the-art weapons. There were no castles in the area, so they had no opportunity to use the boiling oil they had purchased, and this was something they should have thought about in advance. (It was just one example of wasteful military expenditures.) Inevitably, the total effect of the conflict was devastating to both sides.

Aghast at the carpet of bodies extending as far as the eye could see, many agnostics converted to atheism on the field, declaring that there couldn't be a God because no God would allow anything as incomprehensible as this to take place. Other inconsistencies occurred. One agnostic general was caught reciting a mantra during the heat of battle. His penalty was to be summarily relieved of duty, but only after being forced to take off his sword and pants. Then there was an atheist general who cupped his hands in prayer position and thanked the Lord for sparing his life. For that malfeasance, he was immediately burned at the stake by his confreres—the accepted and proper punishment for such an unbelievable transgression.

With the cessation of fighting, the animosities between the two factions were temporarily tamped down, but the inherent problems that had festered for so long continued to bubble beneath the surface, unresolved.

Time passed and twenty years later, in early 839, Tor Thomas, now older and much wiser, conceived a new plan, an ingenious one that called for organizing a children's agnostisade. The idea was put forth to the restive body of replenished Agnostics and they unanimously applauded the idea. "Bravo! Bravo! Bravo!" they shouted in unison. (Better than huzzahs.) Time had conveniently dimmed the memories of the original fiasco, and they rushed to sign up their progeny.

No one thought the children's agnostisade could or would fail because Tor Thomas was again recognized as a truly brilliant thinker and strategist. He had only made one mistake previously, and that was mired in the mists of time. In addition, he was charismatic; a man who could lay hands on people's shoulders and get them to faint and keel over backward (stiff as a board) into the arms of waiting attendants. No other nonreligious person has ever been able to master that feat. He also had the ability to persuade young people to throw down their jump ropes, their marbles, their dolls, and yes, even their gauntlets, and to be ready to follow him anywhere with glorious fealty.

But the children's agnostisade did fail. Sadly, the children were no more capable of besting the infidels (the atheists) than were their elders.

The fortunes of Tor Thomas plummeted as a result of his second foray into nonreligious wars, and he could only find work by going door to door selling coins that he claimed were ninety-nine percent pure gold but on analysis were just nine percent. He was never arrested and tried for his nefarious activities, but his reputation was forever tarnished and he even lost his ability lay hands on people's shoulders and get them to fall backward.

His final days were spent lecturing passersby on street corners, and eventually he seemed to have trouble remembering whether he was an atheist or an agnostic.

Unexpectedly, his ramblings had the positive effect of uniting the two adversaries who came to realize that their differences were not that disparate—that they were, indeed, a band of brothers.

But our history books say nothing about the first agnostisade or the following children's agnostisade. I am confident that someday, the revelation and significance of both wars will emerge. It must. Only the truth can set us free.

A Rendezvous in Jackson County

The location of the Garden of Eden, the land and home of Adam and Eve, is so difficult to pinpoint because there are such varied opinions offered on the subject. The Bible's version is certainly accurate as far as it goes, but it doesn't give us a great amount of detail. It's known that it was located in a lush, green, tropical area and, according to all of the extant paintings, it was a beautiful place, perhaps similar to the Figi Islands, maybe Maui. In the garden were fig trees and apple trees that provided both food, clothing and shelter when it rained. (And it must have rained or else the Garden wouldn't have been so verdant.)

Joseph Smith, the founder of the Church of the Latter Day Saints, revealed that Eden was located in Missouri, specifically in Jackson County, and that has never been disproved. It does bring much joy to all Americans to learn that Eden's location was right in the middle of their country. However, many Missourians insist that Jackson County is not the most tropical part of Missouri.

It is somewhat embarrassing to bring this up, but it is a fact that, in their biblical depictions, Adam and Eve are always wearing fig leaves—just fig leaves—and only enough to cover the definitely required portions of their bodies. This

121

still disturbs many believers who feel that fig leaves are too minimal in their coverage of the human anatomy. A solution to this problem has been proposed suggesting that Adam be shown wearing, say, a Greek toga, and Eve, perhaps a simple gingham dress. The good news is that there appears to be a groundswell of public opinion in favor of this idea. It would be easy for capable painters to add cloting to the existing canvases, and that should please everyone except, of course, the prurient few.

* * * * * * * * * * * *

Here are the lyrics to a song that was written with the intention of celebrating the five thousandth year (approximately) of the appearance of Adam and Eve.

Adam and Eve were quite a pair
Adam was a character
While Eve had more desire than was her share.

> *But nobody seemed to care—*
> *Only because no one else was there.*

Adam and Eve had troubles few,
Taxes never did accrue,
They weren't sailing rockets in the deep blue.

> *There was one thing they did do—*
> *And everyone agrees that was a real boo-boo.*

Adam and Eve felt great elation,
When their lack of hesitation
made them both the founders of a nation.

They say the apple was their motivation,
but here's another interpretation.

(Chorus)
That's love, love, love—That's love, love, love,
Now trumpets wail it, lovers hail it, spinsters flail it, trappers
trail it, brewers ale it, Arabs veil it, detectives tail it, sailors
  sail for it
—That's love, that's love.

Now it is merely my belief,
Adam nearly came to grief
When all he had to wear was just a fig leaf.

Perhaps his outfit was a bit brief,
But no man has ever topped his far out motif.

Till the day Eve met her doom she naively did assume
Original Sin was just a brand of perfume.

Poor Eve, all she wanted was a honeymoon,
Blimey Gov'ner, her problem was having too much too soon.

Adam and Eve are gone and thus,
They get blamed for all the fuss,
just for being socially capricious.

I don't believe their intention was malicious,
Don't be surprised if there invention outlives us.

(Chorus)
That's love, love, love—That's love, love, love,
Now trumpets wail it, lovers hail it, spinsters flail it, trappers
trail it, brewers ale it, Arabs veil it, detectives tail it, sailors
    sail for it
—That's love, that's love.

Thank Adam and Eve—without them now where would we be?

Saint Tropez

When I was eighteen years old, I couldn't make up my mind, should I follow my parents' wishes and go to college, or should I just find a job and get on with my life? That was when it occurred to me that the French Riviera would be the best place for me to reside while mulling over options of such importance.

So there I was on one beautiful, sparkling summer day, sunning myself on a raft that was anchored offshore in Saint Tropez. The sun was lulling me into a state of nirvana when a slight jostling of the raft made me aware of the arrival of a girl, perfectly proportioned, now stretched out alongside me. At first I wasn't certain; was she an apparition or was she real? So I pinched myself and got the answer I was hoping for. I couldn't help but notice that she had on a wet T-shirt and a string bikini, a combination I had never seen in my hometown, Topeka, Kansas. I had seen it in magazines but had never been this close to it—and it was certainly a case of propinquity at its finest.

I immediately made an appeal to God. "Oh Lord," I said, "I have a wish, or maybe several. Will you please put my testosterone on hold until further notice, or at least give me the strength to resist this vision by my side. Or if you prefer, allow me to acquiesce; whatever you think is best."

The Lord elected to deny all of my wishes—or at least to ignore them.

The girl and I were alone on the raft, and before long, she began talking to me in a soothing voice, speaking little French nothings. At least that was how I interpreted them, so I responded similarly in English, and we spent the afternoon getting acquainted in this fashion. All the while, her body was close to mine in what I considered to be natural and innocent, but tantalizing ways.

We remained on the raft until dusk when, in perfect English, she said, "I'll race you to shore." I was better at drowning than swimming but I agreed (not noticing the language switch), and we dove off the raft. She took the lead with long gracefully measured strokes while I struggled to keep up by double-time dog paddling.

When we reached shore, we lay outstretched on the sand as the evening light faded. Then we began to kiss and grapple, while the waves swooshed over and around us, ebbing and flowing under the approaching star-filled sky. I had seen *From Here to Eternity* five times, so I knew the story by heart and was thrilled to be able to assume, in real life, Burt Lancaster's role. At the same time, I was convinced that I had found the girl I would want to take home to meet Mother.

But then, without saying a word, she suddenly jumped up and started running along the beach, beckoning me to follow. I did, and before long, she stopped by an old rusty truck that had some small dolls lined up on the back of it. I began to experience the surrealistic sensation of having become a bit player in a Fellini film, but by this time I was so entranced by her that I didn't know or care what was happening. I recall handing a hundred francs to her, and she in turn handed several of the dolls to me. And that's when she blew me a kiss and disappeared into the night. I didn't know then that I would never see her, whatever her name was, again.

The next day a realization set in when I learned that she was just a clever, conniving little Jezebel who was the daughter of a carnival barker—and that she had sold me three Kewpie dolls at an outrageous price. Another day later, a friend of mine examined the dolls and inadvertently provided the *coup de grace* when he informed me that they were seconds.

I soon returned to Topeka, a disillusioned man. Still not wanting to go to college, I moved into a small apartment and for a while did nothing. But I finally joined the real world again when I landed a job operating a forklift at a Home Depot.

I do that today, and fortunately, I really like the job. Going ten miles an hour on the lift is like going ninety on the open highway, and I enjoy pressing the warning buzzer and watching customers scurry out of the way when I'm delivering a load of five-inch sewer pipes to the plumbing section.

But all is not rosy. While I have been on this job for three years and will probably stay on it as long as there's a Home Depot, I have a problem that's a lot more serious than it might appear. Every night, I have a recurring dream about three Kewpie dolls that come to my door, ring the bell, and then march in despite my protestations. They head for my liquor cabinet and start drinking my ten-year-old Calvado, then get rowdy and won't leave until I give them a hundred francs. They drive me crazy every night.

And when I'm awake, I still can't get the "Deborah Kerr" girl off my mind.

Random Thoughts

It is early evening, and I am sitting cross-legged in my room, contemplating, not my navel, but the navel of an orange which lies incongruously by my side. It has been a cold, cloudy day and my fireplace is lit, crackling, and that comforts me because I still have chill blains as a result of my recent effort to climb the enchanting but daunting Matterhorn.

My ascent of the Matterhorn was singularly difficult, and I recall that I suffered greatly, being out of breath, low on oxygen, and yet exhilarated when the summit finally came within view.

Unfortunately, my lifelong desire to conquer the noble mountain was not to be achieved, on this, my fourth effort. I had no idea I was doing anything wayward, but suddenly, in a moment of intense confusion, five Disneyland security guards, appearing as if from nowhere, accosted me unceremoniously and then quickly rappelled me back to the base of the mountain.

For the next five hours I was interrogated under klieg lights by clones of Grumpy who demanded to know everything about me including my name, address, social security number, and the first four letters of my girlfriend's middle name. Only then was I was allowed to call my lawyer.

I found out later that he hurriedly left home without lunch in order to come to my aid but was rebuffed at the park's front gate because his credit card had expired. Unfortunately, he only had a hundred dollars in cash—not enough to pay the entrance fee and buy a hamburger or sushi.

But now I sit by my fire, out on bail, and my mind wanders across a patchwork trail of random thoughts. I am planning on reading *Wuthering Heights* again because I am older now and the appeal of heaven and the specter of hell loom larger and larger in my mind. I'm sure there would be no *Wuthering Heights* weather in heaven because God would have the climate under strict rheostatic control, comfortable for everyone. And by definition, there is no need for a rheostat in hell—that's an oxymoron, pure and simple. Therefore, in my opinion, it is best that I read the book now because it is not likely to be available in any library or bookmobile in either heaven or hell. I hope you can follow my logic (and the trace of concern that accompanies it).

I don't know why, but this brings to mind Antarctica which is, of course, the antithesis of hell as we know it. I have never been to Antarctica, but I imagine it would be pretty awful to spend eternity on a patch of ice in that region unless one was a penguin or Admiral Byrd. But I do have a friend who was there for five months, and he told me that the only times he felt truly happy were when he pulled his pants back up. I can appreciate that.

It's ten o'clock now, and I have been without any further random thoughts for almost an hour, so I guess I will eat the orange, take a short nap, and then retire.

I hope my lawyer will answer my call in the morning.

Redemption for Politicians

Note: With special thanks to Mark Sanford, former Governor of South Carolina, for giving America a new definition of the phrase "Hiking in the Appalachians," and for being the inspiration of this fictional story.

Hello. I am Governor Harvey J. Moonstruck, and I wish to thank all of my loyal supporters, who—on short notice—are taking time out from your busy lunch schedules in order to listen to an important announcement I wish to make to you and to our great state.

First of all, I want to apologize to my wife, Helen, who is loyally standing by my side—and to my family—and to all of you who I am sure will continue to support me wherever my political path takes me, regardless of any unreliable hints of indiscretions on my part. I hope everyone will remember the good things I have accomplished for our state—particularly the six-lane bridge over the Pisanti River—the Harvey J. Moonstruck Bridge. It is truly a monument for eternity. However, it is indeed unfortunate that the bridge is temporarily closed due to minor structural problems, but those will soon be corrected, I promise.

Right now, though, I am distressed because there are bloggers out there twittering away—claiming that my private life and political life are in complete shambles. Nonsense. They're not bothering to hear my side of the story, so that's why I wish to talk to everyone during this broadcast—straight talk—without notes—even without help from my staff who only learned about this unfortunate ruckus about an hour ago and have not had time to prepare a statement for me to make.

Let me begin by clarifying point number one—only a few of the stories bad-mouthing my good name are even close to being accurate—a miniscule few. Having said that—yes, it's true that I have seen a lot of Vickie over the past six months. She is a hard worker—working day and night—night and day—doing everything she can to help me get our state through these trying times. I cannot forsake her now nor can I forget her silky hair blowing in the tropical bree . . . but what I mean to say is . . . well, um, let me put it this way—the media's claim that I was also seeing Chrystal, who I only saw a few times—with the brazen implication that my seeing Chrystal meant I was not being true to my wife, Helen, *or* Vickie or to Chrystal,---well those are merely politically motivated accusations which should have no place being bandied about willy-nilly in our God-fearing society. Nevertheless, despite my busy schedule, I will try to get to the bottom of all this as soon as possible.

Now, If Vickie is watching this broadcast, I hope she will burn the poems I wrote for her. Although they came from the heart, I admit my poetic style was not really that good, and it's better that they be destroyed than for her to accept the shameless offer to buy them from that scurrilous magazine, "Peek-a-Booty." Also, the two poems Vickie said she liked the most were actually sonnets written by Shakespeare, William Shakespeare, and I'm sorry if I accidently gave her the impression that I had written them.

I never said I was perfect, and what I am asking for at this steppingstone in my career—is redemption—a fresh start—the opportunity to begin life anew with my adoring wife, Helen, who is always by my side, even today. I believe the Bible says that redemption is available for everyone who repents and that seems like the best thing for all of us to do, needed or not, including me.

One more thing—I know that allegations are also going to surface about my alleged relationship with Cindy—and I want to emphatically emphasize that she too is merely a good friend. Yes, Cindy is a beautiful girl—a great natural beauty, everyone agrees, but what I want to make perfectly clear is that her beauty also comes from within—she is a deeply spiritual girl—and at the same time, a very gifted exotic dancer. Most people know her affectionately by her professional name, Tsunami Sue. I hope that her obvious attributes will not cause her to be hounded by the unprincipled paparazzi. I am only concerned about Cindy's welfare, not my own, and the paparazzi should have sense enough not to bother her—or talented people like her.

That's all I have to say about my situation at this time and I am not taking any questions. Thank you, thank you one and all for giving me the opportunity to clear the air so that my reputation will again be considered beyond reproach—as it should be. And now, I must return to my efforts to get the Moonstruck Bridge reopened.

Let me add that I hope all of you will have a real nice day today, and um, by the way, if rumors start percolating about any of my campaign funds being spent on a Caribbean cru . . . um, um, again goodbye y'all.

Her Name Was Hotsy

It's hard to believe, but Hotsy was the only name I knew her by. Well, truth is, I knew her real name was Harriet something because I saw it once on our marriage license, and I was married to her till she died. I never saw the license again, though, because she burned it. I saw her burn it one day when she was mad at me.

Today I'm in jail and I don't know if I'll ever get out, and it's all because of trumped-up murder charges involving me and her. It was in all the papers at the time, at least all the Alaskan papers, although I guess there aren't too many of them.

But I'm getting ahead of my story. It was how Hotsy and I met that would seem unlikely to anyone. I was living alone in Alaska in a small one-room cabin just below the Arctic Circle, north of Fairbanks. I made my living by trapping, and I was just barely getting by, sometimes more barely than others. Nevertheless, I was good at working my traps and snares and going after lynx, marten, beavers, and even occasionally wolves, which were still plentiful in my territory. There was a lot of work involved scraping and cleaning the pelts and preserving them. They had to be in the best condition in order to bring a good price.

My cabin was fairly average for a trapper like me. It had no electricity or water, and the only heat was a small stove that I could cook some things on, and it provided enough heat as long as I chopped enough cords of wood to last through the winter.

I had been living this way for about six years, and to tell the truth, I was happy because I preferred getting away from all the turmoil that goes with being around people all the time. Some folks thought I was brusque and unfriendly, but I didn't think so. It was just my natural way of reacting to them, and I couldn't change that.

Anyway, every month or six weeks I'd have to go into town in order to sell my pelts and to get supplies. After finishing my work, I'd spend an hour or so with a friend of mine. I guess that's what you'd call Gretta, at least she was a temporary friend. But even a half day in town was more than enough for me, and I couldn't wait to get back to the cabin.

All in all, my health was good and my habits were pretty well set into routines, and I thought I could handle about anything. But the winter of my seventh year caught me off guard. It started off being cold, even for me, and I was used to a lot of that. And I knew I should have chopped more wood than I did—hoping for a mild winter, I guess. I started to notice the change in the fall when the leaves fell early and the bears began hibernating before their normal time. Snow also came kind of early, but it was around the first of February when a real blizzard hit. It was worse than any I could ever remember, and that made me feel as trapped as the animals I made my living by. It happened so fast. Snowdrifts started piling around my cabin, and within hours it was more than half way up my door. I worked hard to get my door to open even a little.

It was at the peak of the storm that I heard some sounds, like a knocking, making me fear that a pine might be falling on my roof. I couldn't identify it. Looking up from one of my two windows, I began to make out what looked like a human, and soon after, I could see it really was a person, trying to get my attention, maybe trying to break in, but more likely just to get shelter from the storm. I didn't know. Somehow I got the person, a lady as it turned out, into the cabin and she was near frozen and didn't say anything for a long time. I had just enough wood left to make a small fire and fix her some tea.

She finally recovered enough to tell me her name was Hotsy, and she explained how she happened to get to my place. Her story sounded as unlikely to me as her arrival, but she said she had been mushing her dog sled team, practicing for the Iditarod when the storm began closing in very fast, giving her only ten or fifteen feet of visibility. Then she slipped during a sharp curve, and when the straps of her foot brake didn't seem to work, she lost control of her team and the dogs were soon out of sight. After a few questions, I could tell that she really did know about mushing, and the smell of her clothes supported what she was telling me. I had to go with her story.

Nighttime came (it had actually been dark through most of the day), and I was ready to go to bed, not because I was tired, but just to survive because the temperature was dropping to around minus twenty and threatening to go a lot lower—and the fire was down to coals.

So I said to her, look mam, I only have one small bed, and I ain't about to sleep on the chair. She interrupted me and said don't call me mam. I told you my name is Hotsy. Okay I said. Now—you have two choices, Hotsy, three actually. One, you can sleep on the chair. Two, you can sleep on the floor, or three, if you insist, you can get in my bed, and believe me I'm not recommending that. There are no other options for you except to leave. (Actually, I was afraid she might freeze stiff as a board right on the chair, let alone if she left.) She said she was a resolute thirty-year-old virgin, and she wasn't looking for any funny stuff, so she'd sleep on the chair. I agreed that if she was thirty and a virgin, then she was resolute for sure, but I said that didn't change my offers. By this time, I was under the covers, and it was only eight o'clock. After being on the chair for about half an hour and repeating that she was resolute until I was sick and tired hearing about it—and with the fire entirely out—she climbed into my bed. I discovered that, even with all our clothes on, she had never really gotten thawed out. And my single bed was now really weighted down, and I could feel every bedspring jabbing into me. And she wasn't tiny.

I will say this, having her in bed and being forced to huddle up next to each other did help to ward off the bitter cold. We tossed and turned for a while and actually began to warm up, and to make a long story short, that's how Luella began. So much for being resolute.

Luella (we called her Little Hotsy for a while) was born almost nine months to the day after that night, so that's when I knew she was mine. It kind of surprised me how I took to her especially because I had never had much to do with kids or thought much about them. But she was fun and smart, and even as a little tyke, she liked to play fun jokes on me. For some reason, I thought it would always be like this for us, but in the back of my mind I knew that it couldn't be so—that it wouldn't last. No one though could have predicted how differently things would finally end up.

But nothing was going well at all for me and Hotsy. For a while, in the beginning, we thought we were in love, but we never were, really. We had gotten married mostly for the baby's sake but that didn't make life any easier for us. Not in my tiny cabin anyway. Hotsy wanted to move to Fairbanks where she had lived before, but I told her I couldn't trap there or survive there, and this cabin was my way of life and my livelihood. We would have words on the subject, like maybe ten times a day.

As I said, I'm in jail now where I've had plenty of time to think this over, but it still doesn't seem fair to me. I know things got worse for us, the arguments and all, and I admit I cuffed her a couple of times, probably more, but I don't remember anything else of what happened, especially the poker part of it—so I don't think I'm guilty. I think someone else got into the cabin and did it. Hotsy had a way of making even strangers mad at her. It upsets me that the jurors took less than an hour to settle the issue and not one of them stuck up for me.

Life in jail's not too bad, all things considered. I'm able to use a phone once a week, and I've learned to use a computer some when it's available, so I'm working on trying to learn how to write the story of my life. I may start taking some mail courses. I'll see. It's kind of funny that now I'm in Fairbanks, the place I couldn't stand or even stand to think about—and now my life is easier than it used to be. That doesn't mean I don't miss the cabin.

Even before the trial, Luella was sent to live with Hotsy's Aunt Mable and Uncle Grover, and that was all for the best. She's ten now, and I hear she's growing up like a weed and doing okay. She used to call me when she could and tell me how much she loved me and missed me, but that was when she was six or seven, and I looked forward to it so much. She was the only real contact to the outside world that mattered to me. But the calls started coming less and less often. Last year, she called me on Father's Day and our conversation didn't go too well at all. She was older now, and she started blaming me for everything. She finally said she wasn't going to call anymore and told me not to call her. That was a real blow to me. I keep thinking of her as my sweet little girl and it hurts.

Yesterday was Father's Day again, and it was a long day for me. Every day is long, but this was specially so because I was thinking, hoping, even praying, which I don't do much of, that she might change her mind and call.

But she kept her word.

The Cabbie from Punjab

I jumped into the taxi and yelled at the driver, "Follow that cab!" He responded immediately—"What cab? Where? Where?"

It was just like in every movie I'd ever seen (and I had always dreamed of doing this). I was at LAX, and I screamed, "There! There! The cab right behind you. Hurry!" With that, my driver jammed his vehicle into reverse and crashed into the cab parked just behind him, locking bumpers.

Perfect, I thought, as the two cabbies got out of their cars and prepared to do battle. Being a reasonable sort of man, I stepped between them and said to the cabbie who had been rammed, "Just calm down, sir, because you are the man I want to talk to."

"Who me?" he responded. "Yes, I said, I recognize you because only last week you took me from LAX to Beverly Hills by way of Lakewood."

"Is true," he admitted. "You seem here new, and I thought you enjoy to see beautiful downtown Lakewood."

This man was wearing a turban, and I soon learned that he was from Punjab and that while his syntax was flawed because he reversed words a lot, he spoke clearly and seemed to understand me perfectly.

In order to throw him off balance, I peremptorily demanded that he show me his green card. Instead, he flashed a Costco card. When I told him I wasn't born yesterday, he laughed and reached into his jacket pocket, pulling out his rumpled citizenship papers. Now that surprised me. It was not checkmate exactly, but I had definitely lost a major piece, so I conceded that downtown Lakewood was quite pretty. (I didn't think to point out that there is no lake in Lakewood.)

He told me his name was Bizzari and that it means "haircut" in Punjab. "What a coincidence," I said, "my last name is Haircut." With such common ground, we shook hands and tried to determine if we shared any ancestral relatives. He said he was from Lahore, the capital city of Punjab, and his eyes moistened as he spoke reverently of his beloved city. I complimented his country for its efforts to save the tigers, and he bowed and thanked me profusely but said he was scared of tigers, and in addition, he knew of no tigers in Punjab except at the zoo. His explanation seemed plausible to me, so I suggested that we meet for dinner once a week, always at his house though. I explained that my winnings from lotto were being mailed to me, and as soon as they arrived, I would be able to reciprocate. He graciously accepted my offer.

My friendship with Bizzari blossomed and continued for several months, that is until the night he was preparing his culinary delicacy, *hashli*. While he was stirring the bubbling pot, his turban suddenly unwound and fell to the floor, and he clumsily revealed that he hadn't a clue on how to reconstruct it. (He then admitted that it had been manufactured at a factory in China, and he had picked it up for a song at a garage sale in

Sylmar.) This embarrassment caused our whole relationship to unravel, like cooked pasta falling to the floor. He was exposed; a bona fide fake, not even a fakir, without the possibility of redemption in my mind.

"How could you do this to me," I cried, wounded like a shot bear. "For two reasons," he answered. "First of all I wanted to be one of the hoity-toity Punjabbians." I stopped him right there and shouted---"No cab driver can ever be hoity-toity." Actually, I wasn't sure if I was right, but he quickly retracted his remark and said: "How true! How true!"

His second reason was truly heartrending. He told me that he was actually born in Reseda, but when he was interviewed for a job as a cab driver, he was turned down because he was "too American." So he went to Western Costume in Hollywood and rented an outfit they claimed had been worn by Rudolph Valentino when filming *The Sheik* in 1921. Then he applied some brown Shinola shoe polish to his face and other extremities. When he felt he was properly prepared, he returned to the cab company and applied again. This time, he told the interviewer that he didn't know where Sunset Blvd. was—and was hired immediately. Tears welled in Bizzari's eyes as he told this story and my own eyes began to mist too. I was thinking, in my heart, what a wonderful movie this would make.

But Bizzari's tears were becoming a rivulet, as he stirred the *hashli* and I became concerned that they were changing its consistency. To get him to stop crying, I made a big mistake and promised to reimburse him the four hundred dollars he had paid to have his bumper repaired.

With that, the tears immediately vanished and his demeanor changed into one of complete disdain. In a haughty voice, with arms folded, he accepted my offer and then summarily dismissed me, saying I would hate myself in the morning.

He was wrong about that—it only took a moment.

Meeting Berni Yeller

I have always had a fascination for spoon-bending. In the process, I have spent untold hours practicing it, believing that mastering that single medium would allow me to unlock some of the arcane secrets of the universe. But perseverance did not reward me, and when I recently turned thirty, I reluctantly conceded that I needed help. At about the same time, I learned that Berni Yeller, the acknowledged master of spoon-bending, was living in Fresno, California. That's when I decided to make the relatively short trek from Los Angeles into the heart of the San Joaquin Valley, hoping to meet the guru of my dreams.

Upon arriving in Fresno, I was surprised to discover that Mr. Yeller lived in a very modest tract on the outskirts of town, and when I located his home, I stood in front of it for a long while, deliberating, shifting my feet before finally summoning the courage to go to his front door. It was then that I could hear a fractured rendering of Jack Benny's theme "Love in Bloom" being played on a violin.

When I rang the doorbell, the playing stopped and the door opened. There, standing in front of me and holding the violin, was *the* Berni Yeller. I stammered that my name was

Danny Kerrigan and that my lifelong ambition was to study spoon-bending under his tutelage.

"Come in, come in, Danny, and please call me Berni," Mr. Yeller said, putting his hand on my shoulder in a fatherly fashion while leading me into his home. I noticed how immaculate his living room appeared except for one corner of the room. There lay a stack of bent spoons, pyramid-like, perhaps four feet high.

Berni opened the conversation by saying, "I must be candid, Danny, and tell you that I cannot teach you how to bend spoons because it is a God-given ability that one either possesses or not. It is not a skill, rather it is something that comes from the ethers, the celestial. For me it is easy, but this is hard," he said, pointing to his violin. "I studied with Mr. Benny, you know." Then he laughed, perhaps capriciously, and I joined in but with uncertainty.

Berni then told me that when he was young, his first love was levitation, and he had studied it for seven years. "Did you excel at that too?" I asked. "Well, yes and no," he said. "I managed, through intense focusing, to levitate up to six inches, maybe ten on a good day, but after reaching those heights, for some reason my concentration would vanish, and whoosh, I would come down with a hard landing. In other words, I could ascend well, but I could never get the hang of proper descension, and to be successful, you have to do both, of course. Then, by accident, I discovered spoons, and they became, as Americans like to say, 'my bread and butter.' Or, as you can see by my home, it's mostly bread and not much butter." Again he laughed, but this time, being even more careful, I avoided reacting.

At that moment and without my urging, Berni took a spoon out of his shirt pocket and proceeded to demonstrate his remarkable ability. His friendly mien changed as he grasped the spoon firmly between two fingers. I became transfixed as his eyes began to glow with a fiery intensity while the spoon unmistakably began to quiver and then perceptively bend.

When Berni came out of his trance-like state, he handed me the spoon so that I could examine it before he threw it on top of the pyramid. "I can bend spoons made of any metal except titanium," he said. "Hoo boy, I'll never try a titanium spoon again." Then, as if he had suddenly come out of a secondary trance, he shouted, "Danny, you must have lunch with us."

I protested that I could not impose on this undeserved kindness. But with that, he turned toward the kitchen and in stentorian tones called out, "Honeybunch, prepare an extra plate of your Goulash Extraordinaire—Mr. Kerrigan will lunch with us."

Almost immediately, a small wraith of a lady appeared and nodded a greeting without saying a word. I noticed that she was wearing a gold chain around her neck with a key hanging from it. She walked over to a box on a nearby shelf and opened it with the key, and I could see that it housed her good dishes and silver. She methodically began setting the table, and I felt both honored and humbled by such hospitality.

During our hearty lunch and fortified by a couple of glasses of San Joaquin Red, I had the temerity to ask Berni why, of all places, he decided to live in Fresno. I said that with his unique talent I would have expected him to reside somewhere more exotic—perhaps Kiev, or Casablanca, or maybe even Gloccamorra. (The wine was having an adverse effect on me.) His reply, without elaboration, was that there were a lot of vineyards in the Fresno region and he happened to be an amateur connoisseur of the grape. With that answer I felt it would be prudent to change the subject, so I then complimented Mrs. Yeller on her delicious Goulash Extraordinaire. Her eyes began to moisten perceptibly as she nodded an unspoken appreciation. Suddenly, she thrust a fresh paper napkin into my pocket which I later found had her goulash recipe printed on it and at the end was the penciled word, "Help."

After lunch, I felt it was time for me to go but Berni begged me to stay, saying he wanted me to hear his entire repertoire for an upcoming violin recital which would take place at the Fresno Elks Lodge the following week. With that, I knew I had to leave, so I edged toward the door, speaking rapidly while offering my effusive thanks and apologies.

As we were saying our farewells I could see Berni's wife, again applying the key to the box, this time to put away her cherished silver. And she was carefully counting the spoons.

The White Room

I'm fine now . . . as long as I take my medicine, I'm fine.
If I don't take it, I get mad and I know that . . . so I take
my medicine. It was when I was in high school . . . still in
school . . . that's when I began hearing voices. I'm fifty now,
almost, and today I know the voices weren't real. I know that
today . . . I know . . . but back then, I thought they were real . . .
that people were trying to hurt me . . . that's the way I felt . . .
I became scared . . . real scared . . . too scared to even leave
my room . . . nobody could make me leave it. That's when my
parents . . . they had me sent to this hospital. They didn't say
it was a hospital . . . no one said that . . . I just knew it was . . .
I knew because of the way people looked at me. Some doctors
talked to me at this place and they seemed okay . . . except
they weren't listening to what I was saying. I told them a lot
about myself . . . but they weren't listening. Then a nurse came
and led me to this room . . . it was a large white room. That's
long ago now, but I don't forget it. Never will. It was a large
room and it was all white . . . like it had just been painted. It
smelled funny . . . but not like paint. There were four or five
people in this room . . . they were busy . . . their clothes were
mostly white too. All there was in this room was a bed . . .

and some machines next to it. The bed was . . . you know, the kind they wheel you through hallways on. There were no chairs . . . I don't know why . . . there should have been some chairs . . . but there weren't any. Then a nurse told me to lie down on the bed, and when I did, two men began tying me to it . . . another man started pasting wires on me . . . pasting them on my head, mostly on my head, I think . . . I began to panic . . . anybody would . . . I begged them to stop but no one listened to me . . . no one.

Once, when I was a boy, my older brothers and I were playing in the living room of our home. We were just fooling around, rough-housing, the way boys do, when just for the fun of it, my brothers began rolling me into a large loose carpet on the floor. At first it seemed like innocent fun but I was soon inside the carpet with my hands at my side, unable to move or even to call out. I could hardly breathe and I thought I would suffocate. Before long, they unrolled me and I was unharmed. We went on playing like nothing had happened and I didn't say anything, but nevertheless I was shaken by the incident, and I could never forget it.

The white room . . . the bed in the white room . . . it was like the carpet . . . I was tied down . . . even my head was tied. Then it happened . . . the electricity went on . . . I wasn't expecting it and I started screaming . . . anybody would. I thought it would never stop . . . I couldn't move at all except for jerking . . . I kept jerking.

I'm fine now. I live in this home with four or five other men, and I'm okay as long as I take my medicine . . . but I still think of the white room . . . a lot . . . still do. My parents come to see me here, but not often . . . anyway they're busy . . . I know that . . . I know they come when they can. The shocks in the white room . . . the shocks were supposed to help me . . . maybe they did because I don't hear voices anymore. That's been a long time . . . a long, long time ago. Now there's this man . . . this man that comes to see me twice a week . . . every Monday and Thursday, I think. He's Bob and he's a very nice man and we talk . . . mostly about television and things like that. He always asks me if I'm taking my medicine. I always tell him my story about the white room and he always punches me on the shoulder . . . then he laughs and says—hey, are you going to tell me that old story again? I always poke him back and say . . . hey, I just want to see are you listening . . . then we both laugh. We always do that. He's a nice man. When he leaves I have no one to talk to . . . but I'm okay as long as I take my medicine.

I'm fine now.

My Cousin Jimmy

I was twenty-six, still single, and living in my one bedroom apartment. At that time, I worked in the stock market, had a girlfriend, Cassie, and all in all things were going pretty smoothly—that is, until one day when the doorbell rang.

I wasn't expecting anyone, and I hoped it was Cassie. Instead, standing there was my cousin Jimmy. He was wearing a T-shirt that said "MAÑANA," and maybe I didn't care too much for his baseball cap which was on backward, but worse than that—an ominous observation—he had a suitcase on the floor by his side.

Jimmy smiled and said, "Hyya, cuz, howya doing?" He came forward and gave me a big hug, while at the same time pushing the suitcase with his foot into my apartment. After looking around, he sat down, put his feet on my coffee table, and looked every bit as though he had lived here longer than I.

"What's for dinner?" he asked. I said spaghetti. "I just had spaghetti last night, what else you got?" he said with a laugh.

Son of my aunt Florence, Jimmy was in his early thirties, perpetually in a good mood, but not the kind of guy who was trying to map out a plan for his life—in fact he was clearly going to great lengths to avoid just that. I sensed that my own life would be on hold as long as he was with me, and Jimmy definitely had the demeanor of a man with a lot of time to spare.

The first evening was quite long with Jimmy amusing me with stories about his failed bedroom conquests. Our own bedtime came late but gratefully, and I started to make up the couch in the living room for Jimmy to sleep on. But he had other ideas. He noticed that I had a double bed and said, "Hey, we're cousins—I don't mind if we both sleep in the same bed." After ten minutes going over this issue, it was finally settled—I slept on the couch.

During the night, I awoke, hearing footsteps padding around the kitchen, but I didn't worry about it, knowing that no intruder would open and close the fridge door so many times.

The first week went by with Jimmy just settling, in, ingratiating himself with my neighbors—eating everything in the kitchen that wasn't plastic—not doing much else—while I went to work. When I asked him where he had been before he came to my place he said he had stayed six months with his sister, Brenda—that she begged him to stay longer but, he said he didn't want to impose on her. (On hearing six months, the crick in my neck from sleeping on the couch ratcheted up.)

I was surprised, when, at the beginning of the third week, Jimmy asked me for a twenty (it was actually his fourth request for a twenty), but this time it was so he could take a cab to the Employment Office to look for work. Yes. Yes. When he came home that evening, appearing noticeably sunburned, I asked him how things went at the Employment Office. He said that it had been a beautiful day and the weather man predicted it would not be so nice the following day—so it made sense to take advantage of the good day and go to the beach. He was so honest, and it made sense, at least from his point of view, but he never made another attempt to go to the Employment Office. And of course, the subject of the twenty never came up again.

I began losing sleep because Jimmy liked to sit up late on my couch (my bed now) so he could watch Jay Leno and *I Love Lucy* reruns.

One evening, on returning from work, I first washed the day's dishes and then checked a message on my machine. It was a call from Cassie and she said: "When you know who is gone, give me a call." Jimmy was sitting right by the machine, heard it all, but he had trouble assimilating anything negative. All he did was to smile and say, "Hey cuz, if you've got some spare coins, what say we take in a movie tonight."

Another evening the phone rang, and it was from my Aunt Florence. "Hiya, doll," she chirruped, "how's my baby Jimmy doing, or is he still at your place?" "He's here okay, and he's as comfortable as an old shoe," I replied, needlessly wishing I could have rephrased that. "Well, you take care of him and make sure he takes his heart medicine"

"Heart medicine?" I said, "The only medicine he's taking that I'm aware of are the unmeasured doses of Jim Beam that come from my liquor cabinet." She ignored my scarcely veiled sarcasm and then added, "Well, in case he does have a heart spasm, just call 911."

"Aunt Flo," I replied, "he hasn't done a single thing that could possibly cause a heart spasm, whatever that is." "Beautiful," she replied. "Bye bye, doll."

It amazed me how genetically alike they both were. Well, after all, they were mother and son.

Four months passed and with the arrival of summer Jimmy's stay with me ended almost as abruptly as it had begun. He told me he was going back to Dallas because his sister Brenda knew of a condo he could house-sit for free—it had a pool—and my place didn't. He wanted to know if I could loan him two hundred dollars for airfare to Dallas? Also, he added, hopefully, for another twenty he could buy a new bathing suit.

Believe me, when you can buy your freedom for two hundred twenty dollars, you've got a bargain.

As I was helping Jimmy carry his suitcase to the taxi, he hugged me and said he knew how lonely I was—and he was glad he could keep my spirits up as long as he did—and if I just had a pool he would have stayed with me even longer.

What can I say? He was my cousin and I loved the guy, warts and all. But I won't deny that, as much as I would like to have had a pool, it felt deliciously good to have been deprived of one at that time.

After he left I thought things over and decided that this was a propitious time for me to move. And just to be safe, the only person who would learn where I was moving to—for a while, at least—would be Cassie. We had some catching up to do.

Mistletoe Malaise

Mistletoe Malaise is defined in the Oxnard dictionary as (1) "The uncontrollable desire of men to kiss women," and (2) "The illegal use of mistletoe for the purpose of stealing kisses."

The practice of hanging mistletoe over a doorway, thus allowing a man to kiss any woman who walks under it, originated with the Puritans in the seventeenth century. It began innocently enough as a means of putting a critically needed spark into the long, cold, winter nights. However, the practice grew exponentially, ballooning out of control in the mid-nineteenth century when men of all faiths, and at all times of the year, began practicing this human frailty. Before long, a law was presented to Congress and quickly passed. It is known as the Mistletoe Malaise Bill and although it is a misdemeanor to practice it, studies have shown that 87.5 percent of men still engage in this desultory behavior, the sort of behavior that can lead to further problems down the line. Like prohibition, all efforts to stamp it out have failed.

During the holiday season, the criminal aspects of this matter are normally suspended or dropped. Judges have many parties to attend, and their fortified bonhomie causes them to mellow and be forgiving to their fellow man. But in January, the pendulum swings the other way. Judges are in dark moods (mostly due to holiday-caused digestive problems), and men can expect stiffer penalties in mistletoe court cases.

There is a small body of women who proffer sympathy and pity on these poor afflicted men. They charitably refer to them as kissingly challenged.

Men have a stronger support group available called Mistletoe Malaise Anonymous (MMA). At their meetings, men discuss their problems until they tire. Then they play chess and drink mineral water, believing that this will revive their natural biorhythms and accelerate the healing process.

Not so! They are never cured of this lingering malady. So men of all ages must be watched carefully. Jail time is not a cure; it only gets the culprits temporarily off the streets—and makes them angry.

Police have discovered the source of mistletoe. They know it is imported into Los Angeles from the northwest section of South Bakersfield. They also know it is hauled by llamas treading ancient Indian trails on and over the Ridge Route (the mountains separating Bakersfield from Los Angeles). However, police seem powerless to stanch the flow of traffic despite the fact that the llamas always stop in Gorman (halfway over the Ridge) in time for the Happy Hour.

It is clear that Mistletoe Malaise is not going to go away. (Men are men.) And that means that it is imperative for women to find satisfactory ways of dealing with the problem.

Here are several suggestions that may be helpful to them:

(1) Learn the names and be able to identify the eleven varieties of mistletoe.
(2) When entering a room always look upward. If mistletoe is spotted, quickly turn and flee, or face the consequences.
(3) Always carry a folded umbrella by your side. It is still legal as a defensive weapon.
(4) Have a can of Hot Salsa spray in your purse, ready for use if needed.

About the Author

This is Byron Long's first contribution to the
arena of book publishing. He graduated from the
University of Southern California with
a degree in music and has enjoyed a career as
a professional musician in Los Angeles, California.
He resides with his wife Angela in Laurel
Canyon, an area of the Hollywood Hills that
has a well known and well deserved reputation
for being only slightly askew.

Edwards Brothers,Incl
Thorofare, NJ 08086
28 February, 2011
BA2011059